Bill / Smalley

909 2135582

gpahemsley@
gmail.com

WHAT TIME IS IT?

DAVID WILLOUGHBY

WORD AFLAME® PRESS
8855 DUNN ROAD —— HAZELWOOD, MISSOURI 63042

FOREWORD

David Willoughby was an evangelist. Because of this, eight of the nine messages in this book are evangelistic, the lone exception being "The Heavenly Dove," which was preached at General Conference in Miami, Florida.

Special thanks are due to those who recorded these messages, and who so graciously allowed the tapes to be used in the publication of this book. In transcribing these tapes, and in the subsequent editorial work, only essential changes were made, so that the voice which speaks from these pages will be the voice of David Willoughby with which so many were familiar. Some condensation was, of course, a necessity.

May God make these messages a blessing to the many who will read them.

Arthur L. Clanton

CONTENTS

	Page
Introduction	7
What Time Is It?	9
The Good That Is Not Good Enough	20
Don't Look Back	32
The Woman With An Issue Of Blood	47
Valley Of Decision	61
Not For Sale	77
God's Abiding Presence	90
The Heavenly Dove	103
The Name	112

INTRODUCTION

UNFORTUNATELY, a promising life loaded with spiritual T. N. T. was stolen from the midst of the fellowship of the church of Jesus Christ, November 17, 1973. We do not question the design or the sovereignty of an omniscient God. We do regret that we cannot still share the excitement generated by a ministry that probed deeply, edified greatly, and enriched immeasurably the lives of those of us who had the privilege of listening to David Willoughby preach in his unique, forceful, persuasive, and thought-provoking manner.

The sermons in this book were messages that were preached and tape recorded. They breathe and live. For some strange reason, the works of those who are deceased take on greater significance and added importance. In this case, it can be pertinently stated that death did not add any significance to the powerful thought that is expounded with sincere reverence from a man whose life was filled with prayer, whose heart burned with holy zeal and ardor, whose tongue was truly the pen of a ready writer.

Had David Willoughby lived, and had these messages been printed during his life span, they would have been equally as forceful and meaningful. But because life has ceased for him on this earth, and because his audible voice has been stilled, these documents of truth become especially precious.

David Willoughby was born April 1, 1945, and graduated from Harry E. Wood High School on June 5, 1963, with a four-year grade average of fractionally under perfect. He was a member of the National Honor Society, and was given an engineering scholarship to Purdue

University. The call of God, so strong on his life, urged him into the ministry. He attended Western Apostolic Bible College in Stockton, California, and graduated with high, high honors. He was ordained to the ministry April 5, 1968, in his home town, Indianapolis, Indiana.

He was married on April 25, 1970 to Elaine Reames. To this union was born a daughter, Andrea Ruth, February 28, 1972.

As you read and reflect upon the thoughts of these sermons, and upon the interesting manner in which they are stated, enjoy them to the fullest, and thank God for the special few years that were given to this man to proclaim the gospel he loved with all his mind, soul, and spirit. Cherish the fact that hours of prayer, meditation, and research were poured into these rich pronouncements. The death of the physical man by no means confines the power of the preached Word. "God's truth is marching on." These profound utterances of human thought through the anointed channel, David Willoughby, will live on.

Nathaniel A. Urshan

WHAT TIME IS IT?

And that, knowing the time, that now it is high time to awake out of sleep: for now is our salvation nearer than when we believed (Romans 13:11).

WHAT TIME is it? I believe it is God's will that we know the answer to this question.

Time is such a precious thing, such a valuable thing. It is more important to us than the clothes we have on our backs. It is more important than the kind of cars we drive or the kind of houses we live in. Houses can be destroyed, cars can be wrecked, clothes can get old and decay, but they all can be replaced. Not so with time. That shows how valuable it is. That shows how precious it is. It has no replacement.

We are going to pass this way only once. We're not going back to live life over again. We've got to make the most of what God gives us right now.

Time is not on the market; you can't buy it, you can't sell it, you can't dictate to it, you can't order it around. You can't speed it up and you can't slow it down, neither can you stop it. It is not in the hands of man. It is in the hands of God; He has control of it. No man, regardless of his fame, fortune or position in life, can have control over time.

Time is no respecter of persons. Sooner or later, it visits the well-known Hollywood celebrities and wrinkles their faces just like it wrinkles the faces of people who are unknown.

Death is no respecter of persons. Death visits the rich just as it visits the poor. It visits the proud just like it visits the humble. It visits the well-known and it visits the unknown. Death, like time, is no respecter of persons.

Time takes its toll on all human beings. The writer of Ecclesiastes says that there is a time to be born and a time to die. You can't buy it off, you can't escape from it, when it is your time to go. We're talking about time — something that is precious, something that is wonderful.

James, writing in the fourth chapter of his Epistle said, "Whereas ye know not what shall be on the morrow. For what is your life? It is even a vapour, that appeareth for a little time, and then vanisheth away."

No doubt you've seen water in a teakettle boiling on the stove, with steam coming out of the spout and disappearing into the atmosphere. James said, "That's just like your life." We're not here for any great length of time. People today have the attitude that they are here to stay, but nobody is here to stay. This life is merely a dressing room for eternity. This life is about three score and ten years — so very short. It's just a springboard into something far more serious, and eternal. It behoves you and me to put on the full garment of salvation, so that when we are called out into eternity, we'll be ready to meet our God, and to stand before the judgment bar.

The most important thing in life is not to be famous or to have money; the most important thing is to have a saving knowledge of Jesus Christ, be baptized in His name, and receive the infilling of the Holy Ghost. There is nothing in life more important than that.

We should make the most of what God gives us. We've got to do our best with the time that He has allotted us. He gave His best for us at Calvary, and now it is our turn to do our best for Him. A lot of folks who fail to realize what time it is are not doing their best.

I heard a story about a man who was music teacher in a high school. Late one night he was in his music room all by himself, reading a book, doing some research work, when all of a sudden a bright, angelic-looking being walked into that room. The man was shocked and horrified. This bright angelic being walked over to the piano in the corner of the room, sat down, and began to play beautiful music, tremendously beautiful music.

The teacher was so shook up he hardly knew what to do, and he started to ask questions. "Who are you? What is this? What is your name?" There was no answer, but the visitor continued to play beautiful music, inspiring music.

The music teacher began to notice that this was the most beautiful music he had ever heard. And, in a way, it seemed to be a familiar melody, but he couldn't recognize it. He continued to ask questions. "Who are you? What's your name?" Still there was no answer; the angelic being just continued to play.

Finally, the teacher asked another question: "That music you're playing — what is it? I've got to know; what is that? It's the most beautiful music I've ever heard."

Then this angelic-looking being looked up at him and said, "All right, I'll tell you what song this is. This is the song that you could have composed."

The teacher said, "But I don't understand. Who are you?"

Finally the answer came, "I am the man you could have been."

In a split second of time there began to race through the man's mind thoughts about the past. He thought about the songs he could have composed, and the blessing he could have been. But here he was, an old man with a wrinkled face and a trembling hand, who didn't have the co-ordination he'd had in younger years.

He went home and said to his wife, "I'm not the man

I could have been, but it's too late. I can't go back, I can't
do it over again. That life that is behind me can never
be lived over. It will never come my way again. It can
never be replaced."

I don't want to meet the man I could have been, and
I hope that you never have to meet the person you could
have been. I hope you make the most of what God has
given you.

A lot of people in the Bible thought they knew what
time it was, but they didn't. Why the very Jews themselves, the people of Israel, didn't know what time it
was. That is why Jesus wept over the city of Jerusalem,
and said, ". . . If thou hadst known, even thou, at least
in this thy day, the things which belong unto thy peace!
but now they are hid from thine eyes. For the days shall
come upon thee, that thine enemies shall cast a trench
about thee, and compass thee round, and keep thee in
on every side, And shall lay thee even with the ground,
and thy children within thee; and they shall not leave
in thee one stone upon another; **because thou knewest
not the time of thy visitation**" (Luke 19:42-44). They
didn't know what time it was.

The disciples, themselves, didn't know what time it
was. In Acts they asked: "Lord, wilt thou at this time
restore again the kingdom to Israel? And He said unto
them, It is not for you to know the times or the seasons
which the Father hath put in His own power." The church
age was not fully revealed to them. They didn't understand at all.

People didn't know what time it was in Jesus' day.
When He was carrying His cross up to Calvary, and fell
beneath the load, with the stripes on His back, the women
wept for Him. These were women who had seen His
miracles. "Poor Jesus, He's dying!" They wept for Him.

Jesus told them: ". . . weep not for me, but weep for yourselves, and for your children." He said those words because He knew what time it was, but they didn't.

Forty years later, Titus, the famous Roman general, and his army surrounded the city of Jerusalem. They fought against the city because it had rebelled against Caesar. They cut off all the food supply, and there was mass starvation. Josephus, who was a Jewish historian, wrote an account of what happened. He said it got so bad in 70 A. D. that within the city of Jerusalem parents ate their little babies. They ate their own children, their own offspring.

Someone says, "Oh that's awful; it's a shame that any nation would have to go through that." But go back forty years and remember the words of Jesus: "Don't weep for me, weep for yourselves and for your children." All because a nation failed to realize what time it was.

It is a serious thing when a nation fails to realize what time it is, just as it is a serious thing when an individual fails to realize what time it is. We are living in a nation that has failed to realize what time it is. We are living in a nation of educated people who think they have all the **answers.** The truth of the matter is, they don't even know what the **question** is. The question is: What time is it? They don't know.

They are like that man in the Bible who planned on tearing down his barns, building bigger barns, and laying up his goods. For how long? For many years. They think they know what time it is. They think they're going to take it easy, they think they've got it all planned.

But we can't ordain the future. We don't have the promise of another breath. We don't know what tomorrow holds. We don't know what lies ahead after the next mile, not only for us as individuals but for America as a whole. We don't know what the next year is going to bring. We don't know what tomorrow's newspapers are going to bring. We don't know what the next telephone call is going to bring. We don't know what is going to happen. There might be a flood or an earthquake. We might have a world war on our hands tomorrow. We just don't know.

But I'll tell you one thing: It pays to be ready to meet God, then, even though they do drop a hydrogen bomb on you, you'll just wake up in glory. You'll rise to the new Jerusalem if you're ready to meet God. But if you are not, you'll plunge headlong into the smoldering elements of hell.

What time is it? Paul said, "Knowing the time. . . ." People don't know what time it is. It's a money-mad world. They are tearing down their barns, and they are building bigger barns. They have their plans made, they have their blueprints drawn up. They have time for everything but God. They have time for everything except obeying the gospel. They are leaving God out. That farm-builder said, "Soul, take thine ease, drink and be merry. . . ." But God said unto him, "Thou fool, this night thy soul shall be required of thee."

You can be prosperous in business, you can be successful, you can have fame and fortune and still be a fool in God's eyes. Anybody who willfully neglects salvation for his own soul is a fool.

How will people ever be made aware of what time it is? How can those who attend Pentecostal church services be made aware of what time it is?

Isaiah asked the question, "Watchman, what of the night?" In Old Testament times they didn't have clocks and watches, they didn't have electrical devices to measure time. But one thing they did have was walls and towers that were high.

They would put a watchman on the wall, and this watchman had a vantage point that nobody else had. He could see the daybreak before anybody else, he could see the shades of night falling before anybody else. He was high on the wall. He could see farther over the horizon than anyone.

The watchman had the responsibility of sounding the alarm. He was to blow the trumpet whenever danger threatened. He also made people aware of what time it was.

In these modern days, the Lord has still set watchmen on the wall. Thank God for pastors! Thank God for evangelists who come our way! They are men who know the time, men who know prophecy, men who know where we stand.

What time is it? Ask the man of God. Ask the pastor, ask the evangelist. They will be glad to tell you what time it is. They don't want your blood required at their hands. They want to declare unto you the whole council of God. They want to open the Book up to you.

Someone may say, "If you're a watchman on the wall, pray tell me what time it is?"

Well, it's in the Book. Paul asked the question, and then answered it. He said, "It is high time to awake out of sleep. . . ." It is high time, it is the acceptable time. It's not time to just hear the Word of God, it is time to **do** the Word of God.

Thousands of folks who sit in our churches know the truth, they know Acts 2:38, they know stories about Jesus, they know about baptism in His name, they know the message of the baptism of the Holy Ghost, but they sit there with their arms folded and do absolutely nothing about it.

There is one thing I'm persuaded they don't know: they don't know what time it is. They know the Bible. They know that receiving the Holy Ghost is right, and they know that speaking in tongues is the initial evidence, but they never make a move, they never get stirred, they never cry out to God, they never raise their hands to Him, simply because they fail to realize what time it is.

Watchman, what of the night? Watchman, what of the night?

I preached a revival in Ohio sometime ago, and there was a woman in that church who had been faithful. She had Sunday school pins going back for thirteen years. She had missed very few Sundays in thirteen years, but had never really started for God. The Lord moved in that revival, and on the last Sunday morning of the revival, she gave her heart to the Lord, repented and was baptized in Jesus' name that same morning. After the revival, God filled her with the Holy Ghost, and there was a marvelous change in her life. She finally realized what time it was, after knowing the truth all those years, and not doing anything about it.

It is not time to just know the gospel, it is time to do something about it. It's time to kneel at an altar. It's time to pray. It's time to worship. It's time to get hold of God. It's time for revival, and it's time for a move of God.

"Watchman, what of the night? Watchman, what of the night?" High upon the wall, the watchman is about to give the answer. He has the answer because he has a vantage point that we don't have.

U Thant, the General Secretary-Treasurer of the United Nations, said, "I give the world a ten year-deadline. If the people of the planet earth cannot solve the problems that now exist, within the next ten years the human race will be extinct." Watchman, what of the night?

My home church in Indianapolis, Indiana was going through a time of trial in 1949 and 1950. The former pastor had resigned.

Brother Nathaniel Urshan, the present pastor, was just a young man, and he was so troubled he went for three months without getting a good night's sleep.

One day he got up at three o-clock in the morning to go to the church and pray and seek God. There, sitting on the steps of the church, he saw an old man with snow-white hair. Brother Urshan asked the old man what his name was.

He said, "It's not important what my name is."

Brother Urshan asked again, "What's your name?"

He said, "Well, if you insist, you can call me three-score and ten."

They sat, and had prayer together, and the old man talked to him and encouraged him because Brother Urshan had been going through a terrible time of despondency and discouragement. This man actually laid hands on him and prayed for him. He encouraged him, and told him, "You are the man for this church. God wants you to get this church ready for His return." The man said, "You are going to live to see the Temple rebuilt in Jerusalem."

After they finished talking, he took the man uptown and let him off. No stores or shops were open. Brother Urshan drove around the block, came back, and the man had vanished. He never saw him again.

Brother Urshan said, "That was twenty-one years ago, and pastoring a church the size of Calvary Tabernacle, there have been times when I've been disappointed, but in twenty-one years of pastoring that church I've never once known discouragement. It all goes back to that night in the wee hours of the morning when that man prayed for me and laid his hands on me, and there was a weeping spirit there."

I don't know whether you realize it or not, but an article declares that the Jews have already contracted for 60,000 tons of precut stone for rebuilding the Temple. All of Jerusalem is back in their control. They are about to build the Temple again. Watchman, what of the night?

Can you tell me what time it is? Can't you see the handwriting on the wall? Don't you realize that you don't have much longer to receive the Holy Ghost?

It has been predicted that there is coming a super man by the year 1980, and the whole world will feel the power and influence of this one man. In a vision, every religion, Mohammedan, Buddhist, even Christian, have been seen bowing down, with their hands raised, waving their hands around, worshipping this one man. I don't have any Scripture to prove it, but I feel that the anti-Christ is already born, that he is alive and in the world right now.

When Brother Urshan was in New York city some time ago, he found himself sitting at the same table with U Thant, Haile Selassie, and all those bigwigs with the United Nations. He asked them point blank, "What do you feel is the answer to this world's problems?"

They said, "Reverend Urshan, we feel that the answer to this world's problems is a man. He will have to be an unusual man, he will have to be a super-man. He will have to be articulate, and the kind of man that possesses political magnetism. He will have to be the kind of man that can bring all nations and factions together. He will have to be the kind of man that is good in virtually all fields."

Do you know who it is that they were describing and talking about? They were talking about the anti-Christ. Watchman, what of the night? Watchman, what of the night?

They claim that the pollution problem is getting so bad that within ten years the only way you'll be able to live is by wearing a gas mask.

There is a man who doesn't even profess to be a Christian. He is a scientist, a chronologist, a student of time. This man has studied human history, current events, and the trend of psychology and sociology. He said, "So far as the human is concerned, and so far as my study has taken me, it's less than five minutes until midnight." If a man who doesn't even profess to be a Christian can come up with conclusions like that, friend, how much more should you and I know that time is running out.

Open your Bibles to Matthew 25, where it talks about the midnight cry of the coming of the bridegroom. Those of you who are ready will soon go forth to meet Him. God's time clock is about ready to strike the hour. Jesus will soon descend, clothed in the garments of power. I want to be ready. I want to have my lamp trimmed and burning brightly.

There is no replacement for time. We only pass this way once. I hope that you will never have to meet the person you could have been. You'll never meet that person if you'll obey the gospel and do your best.

What time is it? Hosea answers by saying, "It is time to seek the Lord, till he come and rain righteousness upon you."

THE GOOD THAT IS NOT GOOD ENOUGH

*For I say unto you, That except your righteousness shall
exceed the righteousness of the scribes and Pharisees, ye
shall in no case enter into the kingdom of heaven (Matthew 5:20).*

I WANT to preach on this subject: "The Good That Is
Not Good Enough" or "Why Some Good People Don't
Go To Heaven." Look at it either way; actually, both of
those statements are saying the same thing.

First of all, consider the background of this text.
There was a group of people prominent during the time
that Jesus walked on this earth. They were called the
Pharisees. They were a strict sect, so far as religion
went. They were a disciplined people, so far as legalism
went.

The first thing I want to tell you about the Pharisees
is that they were good; the next thing I want to tell you
about them is that their good was not good enough.

But is not good just good, period? No, there are different kinds of good. There is the kind of good that people
tag on you. They say, "You're good." Then there is the
kind of tag that perhaps you put on yourself: "I'm good."
Then there is another kind of tag that God puts on you.
He says, "You're good." It's not so important what your
neighbor thinks of you, and it's not really all that important what you think of yourself, but the most important thing, both now and when life is all done, is what
God thinks of you.

Let us move further to clarify what I'm getting at.
Let's talk about the Pharisees. They were good. I'm going
to tell you **how** they were good.

They made broad their phylacteries. What are phylacteries? Well, religious men back in Bible times wore leather bands around their arms. Attached to each band was a large box. It was a Scripture box. It had Scripture verses all over it, and a little scroll down inside it. This was a sign or badge, a token of identification to all people. It said, "Look! I'm a priest. Look! I'm a man of God." talk about putting "little" straps on their arms; they wrapped razor straps around them. They put extra large boxes on them, for they wanted everybody to know. "See! Look! I'm a man of God." Yes, they made broad their phylacteries.

They also had their long flowing robes. They were sanctimonious, they were pious, they were really a sight to behold. They were good.

Something else about the Pharisees—they prayed. They not only **prayed,** they **preyed.** How did they pray? They prayed down in the market place. They claim that Thursday was market day in the old times, so every Thursday those Pharisees would go down there. They'd put on their finest religious garb, their priestly finery, and turn out in force.

The Bible says they loved to pray on the street **corner.** Now that is noteworthy. It didn't say they loved to pray in the middle of the block. You see, if they prayed in the middle of the block, they could be seen from only two directions. But when they prayed on the street corners, they could be seen from all four directions. They liked that.

Today, it would be something like this: "I want everybody in town to see me pray. I'm not going to pray in the middle of the block. I'm going right down there to the corner of Fifth Street and Vine, where everybody passing by will see and hear me when I pray. Oh! I have such a burden."

The Pharisees also wanted everybody to know they had fasted. They went around with long, drawn faces. They didn't try to cover it up, they wanted it to be obvious. "I didn't eat today. I fasted. I feel so hungry, I'm tired, and I've got a headache, but I'm doing it for You, God."

Oh, they were good. How good? Good enough to fast two days a week. How many of you fast two days a week? They did. And they were wrong in their hearts while they were doing it. They prayed. Oh how they prayed! They carried their own built in PA systems with them. They wanted everybody in town to hear them. They were good.

The sad part about it was that they were not good enough, because Jesus called them hypocrites seven times in Matthew 23. He said, "Woe unto you, scribes and Pharisees, hypocrites . . . for ye are like unto whited sepulchres . . . you make clean the outside . . . but inside you are full of extortion and excess." That was the Lord's way of making us know they were good, but not good enough.

Jesus said, "Except your righteousness shall exceed the righteousness of the scribes and Pharisees, ye shall in no case enter into the kingdom of heaven." In God's eyes, this was true then, and it is still true today. There is a good that may be acceptable to your community, but it is not acceptable to heaven. There is a good that may be good in your eyes, but it is not good in God's eyes, so it is not good enough. There is a good that's not good enough.

Many people today fall into that category. We have a lot of modern-day Pharisees. They think they're good, their neighbors think they're good, but God does not think they're good. They'll be lost unless they take the only way of escape, and that is through the true plan of salvation.

It is often harder to get people "unsaved" than it is to get them saved. If you don't believe that, go out and knock on a few doors, and see if it isn't true. Everybody claims to be a Christian now. Drunkards are Christians, dope addicts are Christians. It's a popular fad to be a Christian.

I've knocked on doors. If I've knocked on one, I've knocked on probably a hundred. I can tell you before I ever get there what it is going to be like.

"Hello, I'm David Willoughby, and I'm from the First Apostolic Church. We're having a great revival. I'm here, not only to invite you out to the revival, but to talk to you about the Lord, about your soul." So I tell him the Lord is coming again. Finally, I invite him out to church.

"Well, I can't," he says.

"How come you can't come out?"

"Well, you see, I'm a deacon on the church board in the . . . church."

"Oh, is that right?"

"Yes, I've been a deacon over there for several years now. I'd like to come out, but I'm awfully busy."

You know what I'd like to ask him? "What church do you go to? What's the pastor's name over there?"

He would probably say to his wife, "Honey, what is that fellow's name over there? Where's that church located? Let's see, didn't we go there sometime last year? Well, it's over on Sullivan Avenue. Let's see, where is it? Near Johnson Boulevard? No? Well, anyway, I know it's over on that side of town somewhere. We were there sometime ago. I remember, it was at an Easter program."

You think I'm exaggerating? It's worse than that!

Everyone is a Christian now. Everybody goes to church somewhere. Everybody is saved, nobody is lost. That's what carnal-minded people think.

We need the truth, we need the Word of God, we need old-fashioned conviction. Conviction is like a mirror to the soul. It makes us see ourselves as we really are in the eyes of God. Through the eyes of God, and not through the eyes of our neighbors, or through our own eyes.

When the Holy Ghost filled the Temple in the Book of Isaiah, the prophet said, "Woe is me." He saw himself as he really was, lost and undone, and he cried out and said, "Oh God, I am a man of unclean lips." Then God cleansed him and he became a great prophet. I'm trying to say that there is a good that is not good enough.

Many people have the attitude, "Well, I'm good and that's enough." Listen, you'll never get into heaven by trying to pull yourself in by your own bootstraps. Your own morality cannot save you. Your own goodness cannot save you. Your own talents cannot save you. Your mentality cannot save. Even though you are held in high esteem by your community, even though you are held in high regard by thousands, that cannot save you. None of this will merit you heaven.

The Bible tells of a good man who was not quite good enough. We read about it in Acts 10:1, 2.

> *There was a certain man in Caesarea called Cornelius, a centurion of the band called the Italian band, A devout man, and one that feared God with all his house, which gave much alms to the people, and prayed to God alway.*

How many people today have a testimony like that? Very few. Cornelius prayed to God, he feared God, he was kind-hearted, everybody respected him, he was a good fellow. He gave much alms to the people. Friend, if he was living today he would be the kind of fellow who would buy cookies from the Girl Scouts, give to the United Fund, the Heart Fund; he'd even buy peanut brittle from the church folks.

But if you will read the tenth chapter of the Book of Acts, you will find that he was lost, **lost.** He was unsaved, in spite of his goodness. Why? People don't go to heaven because they are good. But if good people don't go to heaven, who does go? Saved people go to heaven. There is a difference. If you are saved, you are good. But you can be good and still not be saved. That's why I say, "Good people don't go to heaven; saved people go to heaven."

We have many people today just like Cornelius. You ask, "Are you a Christian?"

"Oh yes, I'm a Christian."

"How do you know?"

"Well, I go to church every Sunday." That's good, but that's the good that is not good enough. Since when does going to church make anyone a Christian? Does going to a garage make you a mechanic? Does going to a barn make you a farmer? Does going to some athletic contest make you a star athlete? You might be sitting there in a wheel chair. Some of you women who drive into a garage don't know the difference between a spark plug and a carburetor. No, going to a garage doesn't make you a mechanic, going to a barn doesn't make you a farmer and going to church doesn't make you a Christian.

"But," someone may say, "I pay tithes, I fast two days a week." If that's all you do, you're just like the Pharisees. They did this, and were hypocrites. They were lost. There's a good that's not good enough.

What was the turning point in Cornelius' life? It was

when an angel appeared unto him and said, "Send some of your servants down to Joppa to get a preacher by the name of Simon Peter. He will come here and preach to you."

Cornelius did this. And you read in the tenth chapter of Acts that while Peter yet spake, the Holy Ghost fell. You can't be saved without the Holy Ghost coming in somewhere, no matter how good you are.

Peter didn't even get to make an altar call; God "beat him to the punch." The Holy Ghost fell, and they began to speak with other tongues. Yes, Cornelius and the others talked in tongues, and they were Gentiles, not Jews.

The Apostle wasn't through with them yet. He commanded them to be baptized in the name of the Lord.

There is only one way to get into the church of the living God. It's not by paying your tithes, it's not by coming to church every Sunday morning, it's not by doing good deeds, it's not by helping blind people across the street. You can't get into the church in any of those ways. You can't get into the church by shaking the preacher's hand. Signing a card won't get you into the church. Having rose petals dropped on your head as a refined kind of baptism won't get you into the church. Switching your car lights on and off at a drive-in service, and thereby saying, "I have accepted Jesus Christ as my personal Savior," won't get you into the church.

You can do what you want to, but I'm going to stick with the Book. There is no salvation outside of the new birth. You must be born again. Jesus told Nicodemus, "Except a man be born of water and of the Spirit, he cannot enter into the kingdom of God." The Bible commands you to be baptized in Jesus' name and to be filled with the Holy Ghost. Anyone who has been born only once will die twice. Anyone born twice will die only once. The second birth spares one from the second death.

I'm glad I've been buried in the name of the Lord. I'm glad I've been filled with the Holy Ghost. I'm glad I don't have to go to hell. I'm glad there is deliverance through the name of the Lord.

Yes, there is a good that's not good enough. My goodness is not good enough. The only way I can be saved is to have **His** goodness in me.

You ask, "How can I get God's goodness in me?" By being baptized in His name and being filled with His Spirit, that is Christ in you, the hope of glory. Then His goodness is in you, His gentleness is in you, His love is in you, His peace is in you. He said, "My peace I give unto you: not as the world giveth. . . ." But He gives it through the infilling of the Spirit. The kingdom of God is not meat and drink, but it is righteousness, peace and joy in the Holy Ghost.

The first time you were born, you were born into the family of man; the second time you are born, you are born into the family of God. The first time you were born, you were born in sin; the second time you are born, you are delivered from sin. The first time you were born, you were born with an Adamic nature; the second time you are born, you are born with a Christ-like nature. The first time you were born, you were born as a child of man; the second time you are born, you are born as a child of God, and His royal blood will flow through your veins.

Let's go back to the ninth chapter of Acts, and pick up another thought that goes along with this message.

A man by the name of Saul of Tarsus was on the road to Damascus, breathing out threatenings against the church. Saul was a good man. How good was he? The answer is found in Philippians 3:4-6:

> *Though I might also have confidence in the flesh. If any*
> *other man thinketh that he hath whereof he might trust in*
> *the flesh, I more: Circumcised the eighth day, of the stock*
> *of Israel, of the tribe of Benjamin, and Hebrew of the He-*
> *brews; as touching the law, a Pharisee; Concerning zeal,*
> *persecuting the church; touching the righteousness which*
> *is in the law, blameless.*

Would you believe that a man who could say, "I am
blameless with respect to the law," could still be lost in
the eyes of God? When Saul of Tarsus was breathing
out threatenings against the church, even though he
had sat at the feet of Gamaliel, even though he had such
a knowledge of Old Testament Scripture that he could
quote much of it at will, even though he had a lot to boast
of, in spite of all those admirable traits and qualities,
he was unsaved. It is as simple as that; he was unsaved.

There he was, thinking he was right, walking down
the road, saying, "Those Jesus' name people! If I ever
get my hands on them!" Oh he was mad! He was breathing out threatenings.

What happened? Suddenly there came a light from
heaven, shining above the brightness of the noonday
sun. This light was so bright that it actually swept him
off his feet, and knocked him down on the ground. It put
scales on his eyes, and he was blinded for three days.

A voice came to him from heaven, saying, "Saul, Saul,
why persecutest thou me?"

Saul asked the question, "Who are you Lord?" I wish
every Jehovah's Witness could have been there to have
heard the answer. "Who are you, Jehovah?"

The voice came booming back, "I am Jesus, whom
thou persecutest." Jesus says, "When you start kicking
my church, you're kicking against me. That's my body;

the church is my body. It is hard for you (Saul) to kick against the pricks."

"Oh God, what will ye have me to do?"

"Go into the city of Damascus, and it shall be told thee what thou must do."

Saul went into Damascus, and did just what God told him to do. He went to a street called Straight.

That's a good street to get on. Somewhere between here and heaven you had better get on the street called Straight. If you have sin in your life, my advice is straighten up, and get on Straight street. The way to heaven is straight. To get on the street called Straight, the first thing to do is to repent of your sins. When you repent, you're heading toward the blessing of God, because repentance is the first step to salvation.

Saul was sitting there in the house when Ananias reluctantly came to pray for him. He said, "God has sent me that you might receive your sight, and be filled with the Holy Ghost." The Bible says the scales fell from his eyes, he arose, was baptized.

Two days later, Saul was in the Jewish Synagogue of Damascus, preaching and teaching in the very name that just a few hours earlier he had hated and despised.

Nothing less than full salvation can make us good in the eyes of God. Saul was good in his own eyes, good in the eyes of Gamaliel, good in the eyes of the Hebrew society, but lost in the eyes of God until he was born again, until Ananias baptized him, until God filled him with the Holy Ghost. Then he was good in the eyes of the angels, good in the eyes of the Lord. Why? Because it was not his goodness, but it was a goodness that came from a higher source and from a higher power.

You know what stops people from coming to an altar and praying? Is it because they're ashamed of their sins?

No. Is it because they have told lies? No. Is it because they know they have cheated? No, it's not that. It's not people's badness that stops them, it's their goodness. When they start thinking they're good, God can't do anything for them. They have to forget their goodness, their Pharisaic attitude, and be willing to admit they're sinners.

There was a time in my life when I had to admit I was a sinner. Before that, I was lost and didn't know it. One of the world's greatest tragedies is being lost and not knowing it. There are multitudes of people in that category.

Paul was in that category. He was lost and didn't know it. He thought he was saved. He thought he was doing good, that he was doing right.

What is the answer to such a terrible tragedy? There is only one answer. The great gospel light must fall across your pathway, and make you to see yourself as you really are. When you see it, you must be willing to accept it. If God shows you that you are a sinner, then be willing to admit you are a sinner. You must walk in the light as He is in the light. If you don't, greater darkness will fall upon you.

There was a time in my life when I thought I was a pretty good fellow. I made good grades in school, I had a scholarship to Purdue University. Oh yes, I did pretty good. Me, a sinner? No, I wasn't so sure about that. I had never killed anybody. I had never cheated on my income tax. Oh, I'd stolen a few deck of cards from the drug store, gambled a little bit, and indulged in a little off-color stuff, but nothing really bad. After all, I didn't need to go to an altar and weep and pray. But there came a time when God dealt with me. You know what I said, "Listen God, I'm a good-for-nothing bum, I'm no good.

God save me."

Somebody preached a message about Calvary, and, in my mind, I was right there. I saw Jesus hanging there, with blood caked on His hands, blood all over His body, and a big wound in His side. I said, "You died for me." I fell in love with Him right there. I fell at the foot of the cross. I repented of my sins. They baptized me, and two nights later God filled me with the Holy Ghost.

I'm glad He still saves sinners. I'm glad He can save the "good-for-nothing" out of the hog pen of iniquity, out of the quicksand of evil, and put his feet up on the solid rock, Christ Jesus. I'm so glad my hope is built on nothing less than Jesus' blood and righteousness.

My goodness will never save me, your goodness will never save you. I'll never get into heaven on my good opinion of myself. I must ask myself what God thinks of me. Am I pleasing Him? Am I living right, doing right, thinking right, speaking right?

> *Make me what I ought to be,*
> *Help me to be more like Thee;*
> *Bid me come up higher, till Thy face I see,*
> *Make me what I ought to be.*

This verse of song reveals the only way to true goodness and eternal salvation.

Any other kind of good is not good enough.

DON'T LOOK BACK

*Likewise also as it was in the days of Lot; they did eat,
they drank, they bought, they sold, they planted, they
builded; But the same day that Lot went out of Sodom
it rained fire and brimstone from heaven, and destroyed
them all. Even thus shall it be in the day when the Son
of Man is revealed. In that day, he which shall be upon
the house top, and his stuff in the house, let him not come
down to take it away: and he that is in the field, let him
likewise not return back. Remember Lot's wife (Luke
17:28-32).*

THAT LAST verse, the shortest one of the verses
I read, is the key verse because it really conveys the
message of God in a nutshell. "Remember Lot's wife."
There is no U-turn on the King's highway. Don't look
back, but rather look **up.**

The Bible is an open contrast from the beginning to
the end. In Genesis, chapter one, we read about a contrast, where God separated the light from the darkness.
They contrast. They do not coexist; the presence of one
erases the other. Contrasts!

We read in the Bible of a contrast between Isaac and
Ishmael, between Esau and Jacob, between the wise
virgins and the foolish virgins, between the broad way
and the narrow way, between the wide gate and the
strait gate, between the foolish man who built on the
sand and the wise man who built on the rock. So there
you have it. From the Old Testament, carried through
into the New Testament, the Bible is a book of contrasts.

Notice the contrast between two men: Abraham and
Lot. These men were equally blessed of God when they

came into Sichem, in the land of Canaan. Both had the
favor of God on their lives. They were blessed with men
servants and maid servants, with cattle and herds and
sheep.

In fact, it eventually got to the place where it was like
the old expression, "This town isn't big enough for both
of us." That's what it boiled down to. There was strife
between their herdsman. They were so wealthy they
couldn't keep track of it all, for they had a preponderance
of material goods.

It was not Lot, but Abraham, who stepped forth,
though he was the elder of the two. He foresaw a break
between them, and said, "Lot, let's make a decision; you
go your way and I'll go mine. I'm going to give you the
first choice." That's what I like about Abraham. He
wasn't a selfish man, even though he had a lot of goods.
He had the right to make the first choice but he didn't
take it. His attitude was, "Well, Lot, I'll give you the
first choice and I'll just be satisfied with what's left. If
you take the right hand, I'll take the left; if you take the
left, I'll take the right."

There is where the contrast comes in. These were men
of different attitudes. Though Abraham was blessed
with material goods, that is not where his heart was.
Here was a man who drove his tent stakes cautiously,
not too deeply, because he was not interested in this
terra firma. He was not interested in this world.

Where your treasure is, there will your heart be also.
If your treasure is down here, then your heart is down
here. If your treasure is on the other shore, then your
heart will be on the other shore.

Yes, Abraham had great possessions, but he looked
for a city whose builder and maker was God. Abraham
lived from the age of seventy-five to the age of one-

hundred and seventy-five. From the call of God in Ur
of the Chaldees to being laid in a grave in the cave of
Machpelah, for one hundred years, one century — right
on the dot, that man lived life with a faraway look in
his eye.

That's the way I want to live. I want to live life, not
like I'm at home in the world, not as an animal does,
but I want to live like a pilgrim, live like a stranger.
I want to be prayed up, paid up, packed up and ready
to go up.

> This world is not my home,
> I'm just a passing through;
> My treasures are laid up
> Somewhere beyond the blue. . . .

There's a brand new feeling in the air. There's a touch
of heaven that the saints of God can sense. The angels
are beckoning us from heaven's open door. No wonder
we can't feel at home in this world anymore.

"Yes sir, Lot, go ahead, help yourself. I'll take what
is left." Abraham didn't have to have the first choice,
he didn't have to have the well-watered plains of Jordan.
That's what Lot took. Abraham took what was left — the
hills, the rough country, the hard country. So what?
"I will lift up mine eyes unto the hills, from whence
cometh my help. My help cometh from the Lord, which
made heaven and earth." The same God who is God of the
valley is also God of the hills. The enemies of Israel
learned that lesson the hard way.

Here is the contrast. You will either manifest the
attitude of Abraham or that of Lot.

Let's talk about Lot. He was somewhat carnal. The
Bible calls him righteous, but through it all, their was
a vein of carnality in that man. You read it in the Book

of Genesis. He gloated over the opportunity, the privilege of having first choice. The Bible says that he lifted up his eyes and beheld the well-watered plains of Jordan, and the cities of the plains. He said, "That's great, that's for me, that's tremendous." He was the type of man who is always looking for an easy road, a convenient life, a life of luxury.

The Bible says that Lot pitched his tent toward Sodom. Was that bad? Yes, it was bad. You say, "Well, it was just a trend." Yes, but trends are often bad. You know why? Because less than thirty verses from the time it says he pitched his tent toward Sodom, you'll read another verse that says he was **in** Sodom. That shows you why a trend is bad.

We preachers preach against trends if we feel that they are ungodly. You see, God has made us watchmen on the wall. If we see approaching danger, if we see Satan trying to make inroads upon the church or upon individuals, we have to sound the alarm, blow the trumpet, lift up our voices and tell it like it is.

People of God, beware of the spirit that is in the world today. The spirit of lust, the spirit of "gimmie," the spirit of "I've got to have it." I don't have to have anything but God. Take this whole world but give me Jesus.

We have people today who are pitching their tents toward Sodom. They may not be in Sodom but they are headed that way. We have people who are starting to be somewhat hit and miss, and slipshod in their church attendance. They desire a little extra pocket change, they desire to get out to the lake for the week-end. All these little things are trends in the wrong direction. Anybody who puts money ahead of the house of God is guilty of pitching his tent toward Sodom.

Abraham was a type of the person who tries to live

as close to God as he can. This is the contrast. This is the difference. Lot was a border-liner, one who tries to live as close to the world as he can and yet still please God. This is hard to do. You can't serve God and mammon. No man can serve two masters. A double-minded man is unstable in all of his ways. If Baal is god, then serve Baal, but if the Lord Jesus Christ is God, then serve Him.

When the women of our churches start dressing in an immodest fashion like the women of the world, that is like pitching their tents toward Sodom. When they start taking out the scissors and trimming their hair, they are pitching their tents toward Sodom.

But why are there so many rules in the church? Because there are rules in the Bible. Why? Because God wants to know if we really love Him. There must be rules, there must be guidelines, there must be "dos" and "don'ts." How is God going to know if we love Him or not, except we heed His commands? Do what He tells us to do? God didn't say, "If you love me, do anything you want to do." How could we prove our love for Him that way? "If you love me, you will keep my word," Jesus said.

If you stop paying your tithes, you are pitching your tent toward Sodom. When you manifest a spirit of rebellion against the pastor, against the man of God, you are guilty of pitching your tent toward Sodom. It won't be long before you will be in the city.

Bad trends lead in the wrong direction. And rebellion is often a one-way street.

In Sodom, it wasn't long before Lot was affected, was influenced, by his evil environment. The Bible says it vexed his righteous soul from day to day.

Finally, angel messengers from God came to the city

because God had had enough. There comes a time when God gives up. There's coming a time when God is going to give up on this old world, because, as it was in the days of Lot, so shall it be in the days of the coming of the Son of Man. God is about to give up. He hasn't yet, thank God for that, but someday He will.

God sent angel messengers to Sodom, and they preached to Lot. They said, "Pack your bags, get ye out of this place. God is going to destroy this city with fire and brimstone very soon." You would think that, since he was the righteous man the Bible declared him to be, he would have been anxious to pack his bags and get out of there. But would you believe that the Bible says he lingered!

He went and warned his sons-in-law, but it was like a joke to them. They laughed at him. They shoved him out the door, slammed the door in his face, and he could hear them laughing on the other side of the door. He was as one that mocked to his sons-in-law.

Not only had they been affected, but he himself had been affected. The Bible says that the angels hastened Lot because he was too slow about it. Instead of jumping up and taking off, he just twiddled his thumbs. So they got his suitcase and started putting in his socks and his razor for him. They hastened Lot.

Even that didn't do it. The Bible says that he lingered. So the angels went one step further. The Bible says that God being merciful, the angels grabbed them by the hand—two angels leading four people. One took Lot and his wife and the other one took the two daughters. They practically dragged them out of the city. It wasn't any too soon, either. The Bible says that the same day that Lot went out, fire and brimstone fell from heaven, killing all in the city. What day? The same day. They didn't leave any too soon.

As they left the city, they had instructions from God. They were not complicated instructions, they were not hard-to-follow instructions, they couldn't have been misunderstood, for they were simple. He said, "Escape to the hills, don't look back." Now, is that too hard?

Lot kept that commandment, he followed those instructions. And, no doubt, he wanted his wife and daughters to keep them also. As the angels dragged them out of town, Lot, holding on to the angel's hand, no doubt every once in a while would call out, "Honey, are you still there?"

"Yes, yes!"

"Daughters, are you still there?"

"Yes, yes!" There they were, following the angels' leading.

But there came a time when Lot decided he'd better make another checkup. He called to his wife, "Are you there?" There was no answer. He couldn't look back, he couldn't move his head in either direction. He was afraid to do so. The fear of God had gripped his heart. And yet there was no answer from his wife.

Why? What had happened? You know the story. In Genesis 19, you read about it. Lot's wife looked back, and immediately God turned her into a pillar of salt. And, who knows, maybe even this very day, somewhere over in the area of the Dead Sea she still stands there, deaf and mute, a testimony to the whole wide world of what happens to those who look back.

Any man having put his hand to the plow and looking back, is not fit for the kingdom of God. Once you get on the King's highway, there is only one way to go and that is straight forward to that city whose builder and maker is God. Escape to the hills from whence cometh your help. Your help cometh from the Lord. Don't look back toward Sodom.

Why did Mrs. Lot look back? That's a good question. There must have been a reason. Why did she look back? Because she wanted to see the smoke of the fire? No! Curosity? No! I believe Mrs. Lot looked back because, even though she had come out of Sodom, Sodom had failed to come out of her. It is one thing to come out of the world of sin, but it is another thing to get the world of sin to come out of you.

Israel came out of Egypt, but Egypt did not come out of Israel. So what happened? Everyone of them over twenty years of age died in the wilderness except two — Joshua and Caleb. In their hearts the Israelites went right back into Egypt. They said, "Would to God we were back there with the onions and the melons and leeks and the garlic. God brought us out here so He could destroy us." They murmured, they grumbled, they complained; their list of grievances was long. There was one thing after another, one thing on top of the other. And yet they were the ones who had seen the miracles of God. They were the ones who had seen His handiwork.

We have people today who are continually saying, "I want to see miracles, I want to see wonders." Well, write this one down. This may shock you, but it's true. Seeing miracles alone will not change your life. That is the true Bible fact. Many who see them are no better Christians. The Israelites who saw the miracles, failed God. The ones who saw the waters rolled back, who saw the plagues in Egypt, who saw Pharaoh judged, who saw the frogs and the lice, and the water turned to blood, who saw Pharaoh's army destroyed — they were the ones who murmured and complained and groaned.

We're going to have to do more than see signs and

miracles and wonders; we're going to have to cultivate in our hearts a love for the truth, a love for the Word of God. We must make sure that we are faithful, rooted and grounded, steadfast and immovable.

Miracles alone don't change peoples lives. They don't perfect anybody. Think of all the miracles Judas saw, think of all the miracles Demas saw. They lost out. After once having followed the Master, they looked back.

Another example to illustrate looking back would be that of Abner, captain of the host of Israel. Abner killed Joab's brother, Asahel. And Joab harbored a grudge and a bitterness in his heart. He said, "If I get a chance, I'm going to get even with him." Joab was deceptive. He was the type who went around like Absalom, embracing the men of Israel, and smiling.

Abner had fled to Hebron because that was a city of refuge. A city of refuge was appointed in Israel, so that whenever a man killed another man in self defense, he could flee to the city of refuge. If he stayed there as long as the high priest lived, he had safety in the city of refuge.

Joab followed Abner to that city of refuge, Hebron, and he got just outside the gates. He didn't go in, he stayed just outside the gates, and there he smiled and put on a big show. He sent one of his servants, and said, "Tell Abner, the captain, that I want him to come out here and have a special meeting; I want to see him."

Would you believe it! That man, a man of integrity, a man who should have known better, a man of knowledge, a man who had a military keenness about him, just nonchalantly walked out the gate of the city of refuge. Joab threw his arms open wide, apparently to welcome Abner, but while they were embracing one another, Joab took his dagger out, smote Abner under the fifth rib, and he fell over dead in his own blood.

When king David heard about it, he threw up his hands and said, "Oh, Abner, you died as a fool dieth. Your hands were not bound. You were not as a captive being carried away, as a prisoner to a foreign land. You died as a fool dieth." So close to the city of refuge, so close to safety, yet he might as well have been a million miles away. So close, yet so far.

Why did he die as a fool dies? Because he looked back. He looked back! He made the same tragic mistake that Lot's wife made in respect to Sodom. She looked back.

If we expect to be saved, we have to get into the king-dom and stay in the kingdom. We must keep looking forward.

When God's people of Israel entered Canaan, one of the first cities they came to, and conquered, was Jericho. The whole city was destroyed by God. Right? Wrong! There was one house that had a scarlet colored rope hanging out the window. This was Rahab's house. Rahab had been a harlot. So what? Jesus told the Pharisees that the harlots would beat them into the kingdom of God, because they would repent.

God's instructions, through the spies, was this: "Rahab, get in your house, and bring in everyone you want to be saved. Take your family, make sure they are in the house. Don't let them come out, once they are in, because if they come out of the house that has the scarlet rope hanging out of the window, we will not be responsible for taking their lives. So long as they stay in the house, not one hair on their head will be touched." If any aunt, uncle, cousin, grandma, or grandpa had been in the house, and then had decided, "I'm going out of the house," when the battle and the siege was in progress, they would have been caught outside, and would have been cut down by the sword of God's army. Once they got in the house, they had to stay inside.

Once you decide to walk with God, you have to make a consecration. Just like Elisha, you had better go back and kiss mom and dad, then burn the plow and sacrifice the oxen, because you have a new walk, a new profession, a new road, a new family, a new father, new brothers, new sisters, and a new way of living. You are a new creature in Christ Jesus. Old things pass away, and behold all things become new.

When you come to God, there is no past. There is nothing but a present. Paul said, "Forgetting those things which are behind, I press toward the mark for the prize of the high calling of God in Christ Jesus."

When you come to God, you have to burn the bridges. Take a match and burn them down. You have to cut some ropes, cut some strings. You not only have to get out of Sodom, you have to get Sodom out of you. You not only have to leave a world of sin, you have to make sure it has left you. Burn the bridges!

When I came to God, there were some consecrations that had to be made. I had to write some checks. Why? I wanted to have a clean slate. I didn't want to owe this old world a dime. My decks of cards went right into the trash can. What was I doing? I was burning bridges, I was cutting ropes, I was going on. There wasn't any looking back, no going back.

There isn't any retreat in the army of God. The only way to make it is in the front lines. He gave us a helmet, he gave us a sword and He gave us a shield, but He never gave us any protection for our backs. There is only one way to be victorious in the army of the Lord and that is to stand straight and go forward for God.

I used to be quite a sports enthusiast before I received the Holy Ghost. I was involved in sports a lot, and even the ones I wasn't involved in, I went to see them, because I was interested in them. Basketball! I went to twenty games out of twenty before I received the Holy Ghost, and that season I went to zero out of twenty. What was I doing? Cutting the ropes. I traveled another road, I started a different direction. I'm not looking back, I don't want to look back.

I used to have close to $300 worth of rock music. I was quite a fan of popular music. I had a record collection that I took pride in. It had a lot of big-name performers in it. I knew records like I knew my name. But there came a time when I took all those records, one at a time, read them, broke them and threw them into the trash can. Did I weep and cry? No, I shouted and glorified God. Some young teenager might have come running out of the house and said, "Why didn't you give them to me?" No, I was burning a bridge, I was cutting the rope, it was going to stop right there. These things were going to go no further.

Someone may say, "you burned so many bridges that it made you restricted and narrow minded?" Ah, listen! I want you to know, I'm more free and have more liberty than I have ever had in my life. Jesus set me free, and made me free indeed. I'm not in jail, I'm not in prison. It's people who do those kind of things I used to do that are. They are on the wrong side of the bars and I'm on the right side. I have no desire to be where they are. I have already been there. But praise God, when I was in jail, Jesus came and went my bail.

I want to be like Abraham, I don't want to drive my stakes too deep. Thank God, I want to be guilty of having a faraway look in my eyes. I want to be looking for that city whose builder and maker is God. I don't want to be like Lot.

Mrs. Lot looked back because, in her heart, she was still in Sodom. Israel looked back, because in their hearts they were still in Egypt. What is in your heart? Is there a strong desire to draw nigh to God, or is there a desire to try to live as close to the world as you can and still get by? Who are you trying to live like? Which part of the contrast are you? Are you following Abraham or Lot? What are you looking at? Do you have dollar signs in your eyes, or do you see a city ahead? Are you looking on the glitter and the glamor and the attractive allurements of this old world, or are you looking away to a city on yonder shore that is reserved for spiritual pilgrims and strangers who have proved faithful along life's way?

We are living in a day of the artificial. Flowers are artificial. The front of a building may look like it's brick, when it is really just an outward veneer. Is there anything real anymore?

There is such a thing as artificial Christians and artificial Pentecost! But we cannot depend on outward appearance. We are going to have to have the goods in our hearts. Pentecost is not a story that is told. It has to be a life that is lived in the fear of God. It is possible to be so close to church and yet so far from God. If we expect to be saved, we're going to have to do more than just fill up space on a church pew. We're going to have to do more than just sing three songs every church night, listen to prayer requests and testimonies, or even take part in the altar service. There is going to have to be more than the planned program of man. There must be a personal, Bible-based experience with God.

There was a young man in my home church in Indianapolis. When he came to God, he was in such a wretched condition the doctors had given him up to die. He had to be carried back to the prayer room with his arms draped around the shoulders of the other men. The man had been on dope, and his body was almost ruined by it. God healed him, touched him, he was baptized in Jesus' name, and filled with the Holy Ghost. The man seemingly loved the Book. He brought others to church, and his life was a beautiful testimony.

Several years later, while I was out in California preaching, a report came to me: "Did you hear about Brother Jimmy?"

"No, what?" I asked.

"He's quit going to church."

I said, "Oh no! You don't mean the Jimmy that studied his Bible, and used to bring even people of other cults and denominations out to church. The Jimmy who said, 'No, I don't ever want to go to hell.' You don't mean that Jimmy do you?"

"Yes, I'm afraid he's looked back."

My! I just couldn't believe it, I couldn't understand.

I was still out in California a few months later when another report came to me. "Did you hear about Jimmy? There were some boys gambling in the basement of a house in Indianapolis, and some other boys who hated them lined them up against the wall and robbed them at gunpoint. While the holdup was in progress, Jimmy, not knowing what was going on, just stumbled in. He knew one of the men who was holding up the card party, and he called him by name. This threw the man into a scare, and he turned around and shot Jimmy. He fell over, and then he shot him twice more in the head."

When that report came to me, an awful feeling swept over me. I thought, "Dear God, here is another testimony telling us that it doesn't pay to make a U-turn on the King's highway.

The wages of sin is death. There is no **looking** back if

you burn the bridges. There is no **going** back if you burn
the bridges. If you make the act of consecration that says
there is only a forward gear, and no reverse gear in the
King's chariot. The chariot of God and the horses of God
move only in one direction, and that is toward that
eternal city, taking its riders into the pearly gates.

This is no time to look back, but rather the time to
look up, for our redemption drawth nigh. I believe we
are living on the verge of the coming of the Lord.

As it was in the days of Lot, so shall it be in the days
of the coming of the Son of man. All the signs are nothing
but guideposts, pointing us to the goal, and making us
know that we are not on a practice drill, but in the real
race. We have come around the last turn, and are on the
home stretch. We are nearing the finish line.

Remember Lot's wife. She started for the mountains,
just as Lot did, but she lost everything because she
looked back.

Keep your face set toward that city whose builder and
maker is God, and **don't look back.**

THE WOMAN WITH AN ISSUE OF BLOOD

And a certain woman, which had an issue of blood twelve years, and had suffered many things of many physicians, and had spent all that she had, and was nothing bettered, but rather grew worse, When she heard of Jesus, came in the press behind, and touched his garment. For she said, If I may touch but his clothes, I shall be whole. And straightway the fountain of her blood was dried up; and she felt in her body that she was healed of that plague (Mark 5:25-29).

LET US begin by looking at the situation of this woman who had suffered an issue of blood for twelve years. During those twelve years she was not idle, but went to many physicians—to this doctor and that physician, and still suffered in her body, with no relief. The Bible says that at the end of those twelve years, she was the nothing better.

To make bad matters worse, she had spent all her money going to doctors. You can understand that when you stop and think about how much they charge now. You can go broke going to doctors. That's what happened to her, and still they couldn't help her. That proves to us that man is limited.

Did you know that doctors take an oath called the Hippocratic oath? According to that oath, they practically swear that they are going to do their very best to preserve life, even if it means staying up day and night. There have been times, through medical operations, that they've had to just about do this to save a life. But in spite of their best efforts, in spite of the fact that their hair is matted and sweat is on their faces, in spite of the

47

fact that their hands are skilled in training through years of study and practice, there comes a time when, in their frustration, they hold an X-ray up in the air, and shake their heads saying, "I'm sorry, we have gone as far as we can go." Man is limited, doctors are limited, medical science is limited in what it can do.

But I serve a God that can do anything. I serve a God who begins when man stops. I serve a God who specializes in hard things. Is any thing too hard for God?

> *Got any rivers you think are uncrossable?*
> *Got any mountains you can't tunnel through?*
> *God specializes in things thought impossible,*
> *And He will do what no other power can do.*

With man, many things are impossible. But not with God, for it is said, ". . . with God all things are possible." I serve a God who has all power.

This woman was nothing better but rather grew worse. She was at the end of the line, at the end of the rope. Not only had the disease itself taken a toll upon her, but there began to set in that spirit of helplessness which said, "There is no way, no help, for you."

Think of the time she was living in. For four hundred years in Israel there had been no prophet, no man of God, no dream, no vision. That period is called the silent time between the Testaments. John the Baptist came on the scene after four hundred years, but even under his ministry there was no healing virtue. This woman had nothing to look forward to. It seemed that every door had been slammed in her face.

But one day, perhaps while she was out in the backyard, sitting on a stump, with her lower lip hanging down, feeling sorry for herself, a neighbor who had heard about Jesus said, "Say, I've got some good news for you!

That stranger from Galilee who is going about doing good —let me tell you several things He's done. There was a blind man on the road to Jericho, by the name of Bartimaeus, and God opened his eyes—just like that! They claim that in the Temple the other day there was a man with a withered arm, and Jesus said, "Stretch it out." About that time he had it out level with his body, his withered arm was healed. And let me tell you about the time there were ten lepers, and He cleansed all of them— just like that?"

When she heard those stories about Jesus, faith welled up in her. And that neighbor was so glad that he could tell her, "He's in town right now."

For the first time in months, a great smile came on her face, and a twinkle came in her eye. Something told her, "This is it! This could very well be my chance of a lifetime. The doctors couldn't do me any good. But now I've heard about Jesus."

She made a great statement of faith. She said, "I know. . . ." She didn't say, "Well, I think maybe it could be," but, "If I can but touch the hem of His garment, **I shall be** made whole." That was a strong statement of faith.

There was more to her faith than just making a statement. She did something about it. She got up and started for Him. She said, "If He's in town, I want to find Him."

Finally she located Him. The only trouble was that when she got where He was, there was something that separated her from Him. You know what it was? It was a crowd of people. When you get down to business with God, and purpose in your heart that you're going to touch Jesus, you've got a battle on your hands. I've found that out the hard way. This woman didn't just walk right up, and get healed in an easy manner. There was a struggle involved.

The Bible does not go into great detail; it does make us know that she had to go in through the press. Now think of this: The woman was weak and frail. The disease that had been coursing through her for twelve years had sapped her strength. But in spite of her weakness, she still had to struggle to move through the crowd, and elbow her way beyond the bodies. No doubt people stared at her, thinking "Woman, you're acting crazy, you're acting odd." But they didn't know that way down deep in her heart she had a burden, way down deep in her heart she had a desire to touch the hem of the Master's garment.

Probably there were times when she got close, but someone came between her and Jesus, maybe pushed her back or shoved her down. But even though she suffered some setbacks, her faith remained constant, her faith remained strong. No doubt she had to try several different avenues of approach, several different ways.

Finally, after the struggle, after the fight, after the battle (you might call it), the Bible says, she stretched out her hand and touched the hem of His garment. And as soon as her finger tips touched the hem of His garment, the Bible says that immediately, not two weeks later, not five days later, not even ten minutes later, but immediately, virtue went out of Jesus through those garments, came into her body and she was healed. Healed! What the doctors couldn't do in twelve years, Jesus did in a split second. Isn't that wonderful?

That's not all. Not only was she healed but something else happened. Jesus, who had been walking by the wayside, came to a sudden halt. He looked around and said, "Who touched my clothes?"

Peter was standing there, and said, "Well, that's a peculiar question. There are people all around you, bumping into you. What do you mean?" He wasn't getting the gist of the whole thing.

The Lord spoke to him and said, "Somebody has touched me: for I perceive that virtue has gone out of me." Then He looked around about, and there was the woman. She came, fearing and trembling, and fell on her knees, saying, "Lord, I was the one who touched the hem of your garment."

Jesus didn't rebuke her, He commended her. He loved her. I like what He said to her. I like the very first word that came out of His mouth. The Bible says He said unto her, "Daughter. . . ." She was probably older than He, for He was crucified at the age of thirty-three. Do you know why He called her daughter? Because He was the Father. Oh, yes sir! Philip said, "Lord, show us the Father, and it will suffice us." Jesus answered, "Have I been so long time with you, and yet hast thou not known me, Philip? He that hath seen me hath seen the Father; and how sayest thou then, Shew us the Father?" (John 14:9, 10).

"He that hath seen me hath seen the Father." I believe that Jesus Christ was God manifest in the flesh. He was God the Father in a fleshly encasement. He had the power to prove it, the power to do the job when it needed to be done. He said, "Daughter, thy faith hath made thee whole; go in peace, and be whole of thy plague."

Oh, I'm glad for the hem of His garment. We sing that song, "If I could but touch the hem of His garment." But some people don't seem to know where the hem of His garment is located. The hem of the garment is not up high; it's way down low. It's exactly opposite of where we often think it is. You don't go **up** to touch God, you must go down.

Some people who come to church during revival want

to touch God, but they want to do it on their terms. They want to do it their way. They don't want to have to eat humble pie, so they just come and put forth a little minor effort on their own levels.

But the hem is not up at the shoulders. In fact, the hem is not even at the waist. In Bible times, the men wore garments with hems practically on the ground. Therefore, let's put two and two together. This makes us to know that the woman, in order to touch the hem of His garment, had to humble herself. Perhaps she had to get down on all fours, and crawl like a dog through the dust and the dirt, in spite of what the crowd thought, in spite of what they said about her. She wasn't afraid of them. She had only one goal in mind: "I've got to touch the hem of His garment." She humbled herself, she reached out, she touched my Lord, she touched my Jesus, and He did something great for her.

If there is a need in your heart and life, if the doctors can't help you, if you're nothing better, but rather have grown worse, I want you, in your time of desperation, to take hope and courage, for there is a King named Jesus, there is a great physician, who is able to heal all manner of sin, illness, ailments and sickness. I serve an all-powerful God, an almighty God. There is nothing too hard for Him. Aren't you glad this woman was healed? Isn't it wonderful?

Look at verse 24 again. It says, "And Jesus went with him; and much people followed Him, and thronged Him." Here's when we come to a point in this message that I believe God wants brought out. Possibly you've never noticed this before. You see, most preachers who speak on this portion of scripture, talk about the woman who touched the hem of His garment. But what I have said up till now was merely to lay a foundation for what I'm about to say.

I want to take the spotlight off the one who **did** touch the hem of His garment, and focus it on the crowd of others who **didn't.** Jesus walked by the wayside. A crowd of people surrounded Him — some were right beside Him, some were right in front of Him, some were right behind Him; they thronged Him. And many of them had needs just as great as the woman's. They had afflictions as bad as hers. They had spiritual ailments, as well as physical. They had mental problems, as well as financial problems. It would be hard to tell what kind of needs were there in the crowd. Yet, at the same time, there was enough power in Jesus' garment to heal every cancer, every heart trouble, and to meet every need — physical, spiritual, mental, or financial in the whole wide world. The power in those garments was great, and the need in that crowd was great, but nobody was tapping the source. Jesus kept walking. He was walking right through their city. There He was; they were close to Him. But nobody was touching Him with faith.

The woman came from the outside, touched the hem of His garment, and stopped Him from walking. She stopped Him right in His tracks and brought the rest of them to an open shame.

This was a different kind of touch. This was a touch of faith. It's one thing to touch God but it's another thing to do it with faith. You can touch Jesus, but make sure you have some faith when you do it. That's when the good is accomplished, that's when the deeds are done. Otherwise, nothing is accomplished. Faith makes all the difference in the world.

That whole crowd was guilty of cheating themselves. They didn't get a thing. The Bible tells us that one little woman got what she was after, but we can't find any-

where in the Bible where the others even got as much as
a tiny, little blessing from God. They stood there dumb-
founded, puzzled by it all, and cheated themselves.

The Bible says, "Blessed is the man that walketh not
in the counsel of the ungodly, nor standeth in the way of
sinners. . . ." And on that day that's all that some were
good for—just to stand in the way of sinners.

Some were spectators. They just came to look. "Oh yes!
That's Jesus. He's not much to look at, is He?"

Then there were others who came to gossip. "Can any
good thing come out of Nazereth?" They never bothered
to try to find out for themselves. All they wanted to do
was to spread a lot of gossip. "Any good thing! Isn't that
the carpenter, the son of the carpenter, Joseph?"

Some came to hear, to catch some words out of His
mouth, so they could report Him to the Jewish police and
get Him into trouble.

But while some came to listen, and some came to talk,
and some came to look, there was one little woman who
came to **touch.** She was an example for everyone of us.
She came with a right attitude, with a right motive, with
a right desire.

When we come to church we shouldn't come just to be
entertained, we shouldn't come just to go through a plan
or a ritual or a ceremony, we shouldn't come just to be
spectators. We ought to come, not to talk or visit with our
neighbor, but to glorify Jesus Christ.

I am afraid we have a lot of people who have just been
walking near Jesus. They have been right in front of Him,
they've been right beside Him, or they've been right
behind Him. They have followed Him, they've been
thronging Him, but yet they have failed to really touch
Him over the years.

When you have revival today, the "Tator" family is

liable to show up. There is Agi**tator,** Dic**tator,** and Spec**tator.** And the worst one of them all is often Spec**tator.** We have some people who, even though God is moving in a great way, are satisfied to sit back, kind of grumpy, and criticize those who are trying to get hold of God. They are critical of those who are worshiping the Lord. "Why I wouldn't act like that; you couldn't **make** me act like that." It's people with attitudes like that who don't touch the hem of His garment. They are going to miss the rapture. They are going to miss God.

Pentecost is not intended for spectators. Pentecost is intended for participators. Pentecost isn't like a show where people sit back and watch a movie on the screen. Pentecost is something you get into yourself. You're not coming to watch a cast of actors on the stage, you're coming to be an "actor" yourself, front and center.

We have a lot of people who are allowing themselves to be cheated at heaven's gate. That's what the church is—the gateway of heaven. The church is Bethel, which means "the house of God." This is where decisions are made, this is where destinies are determined. This is where we say, "Yes" to Jesus. This is where our souls are blessed. This is where we have communion together, and enter into the kingdom of God, filled with the Holy Ghost. The house of God is the gateway to heaven. That's what Jacob called it when he had dreamed of the ladder reaching up into heaven. He said, "God is in this place, and I knew it not." I want you to know that God is in this place, whether you know it or not.

Do you know what stops a lot of people from getting revived? It's because they come to church with the wrong mental attitude. They sit back in their seats and say, "Well, Lord, if you want me to shout or if you want me to speak in tongues I want you to drop a bombshell right in my lap. Knock me out of my seat." The revival ends, and they're still sitting there.

Jesus knew what street that woman lived on. He knew her house number. But He didn't go to her house; she had to go to Him. Too many people are waiting for the Lord to come to them. But this woman got stirred up. She put on her sandals and her clothes, got out of her house, and started hunting Him. She walked the cobblestone streets of that city, then pressed her way through a crowd of onlookers and spectators, and finally reached down and touched the hem of His garment.

Mental attitude will make the difference, one way or the other.

The Bible has many accounts of those who cheated themselves.

One of these is found in the parable of the prodigal son. Remember how that son wasted his father's inheritance living in sin? When he came home, his dad was so happy that he threw a big party. They killed the fatted calf. They put a ring on his finger, dressed him in a new robe, and gave him new shoes. All his friends were invited to the homecoming celebration.

There was another son — an elder brother. He is seldom mentioned in our preaching. This son never backslid. He never wasted his father's goods. He stayed at home, faithfully walking behind the plow, working in the fields.

When the prodigal son came home, the elder brother heard about it. When he came in from the field, he heard the sound of music and dancing. He stopped one of the servants, and asked, "What's going on in there?"

The servant said, "Haven't you heard? Your little brother's come home, and they've killed the fatted calf for him. They're having a big party for him."

The Bible says the elder brother was angry. He sat

down and would not go in. He was mad; mad at his brother, mad at his dad, mad at the world, mad at himself, mad at everybody.

His dad came out and said, "Son, I've heard that you're not going to come into the party and rejoice with your younger brother. What's wrong?"

The son said, "Listen Dad! I've been here all the time. I've never once failed you, I've never once committed adultery, I've never once gone into sin. Yet you have never once thrown a party for me. But that sinful brother of mine came home, and you threw a party for him." Oh, he was angry! He had an envious attitude.

Do you know what his dad told him? He said, "Son, thou art ever with me, and all that I have is thine." He had received not because he had asked not. Friend, it was there under his nose all the time. All he had needed to say was, "Dad, let's have a party," and his dad would have said, "All right, let's have it." He had cheated himself by his own carnal, foolish attitude.

Let me show you how that scene **could** have been enacted. Picture the elder son coming in from the field.

"I hear music and dancing. What's going on here?"

"Haven't you heard?" the servant asked. "Your brother's come home."

"You mean my little brother's really come home? And they're having a party for him? Am I invited too?"

"Sure, come on in and have a big time. There's plenty of fatted calf for everyone."

See how his attitude made all the difference in the world. He could have gone in and rejoiced with them, but he sat out there on a stump and felt sorry for himself, and angry at everybody.

Sometimes sinners come in out of a cold dark world and, in one night, touch God. This makes some supposedto-be religious people envious. They sit back, grumpy, and say, "God never blessed me like that." No wonder! They're sitting out there on the "stump of carnality," wrapped up in a shell of pride. They need to let go, and let God have His way. People will never outgrow their need for touching the hem of His garment. They'll never outgrow their need for letting the waters of the Holy Ghost bubble up from within.

Some people have the attitude that the blessing of God depends upon the singing of a certain song, or the preaching of a certain message. That is not true. If, on any given night, you do not touch God for yourself, there's nobody to blame but you. You can't blame the pastor or the evangelist. It depends upon your hunger and your attitude.

They say that if you lead a herd of horses to water and none of them drink, something is wrong with the water. But if you lead a herd of horses to water and some of them drink, while others don't, there's nothing wrong with the water; something is wrong with the horses that don't drink. During a revival, you'll find two groups: those who will drink of the Spirit and those who won't. And those who won't are spectators. They're trying to get out of Pentecost only its fringe benefits.

It won't work that way. You've got to worship God with all your soul, with all your mind, and with all your strength, and take the opportunity to touch Him for yourself. You must work out your own salvation with fear and trembling. You can't get into heaven on somebody else's blessing.

If you want to touch God, you can. I can't tell you what songs were sung on the night I received the Holy Ghost. I can't tell you how the service went. And for a long time I couldn't have told you who preached, or what was preached. (They had to tell me later who it was and what he preached; I had forgotten.) All this didn't mean that much. That makes me know that it's not just what song is sung or what message is preached. It's a matter of having a personal desire, an inward desire, just as that woman had; something that makes you say, "I don't care who's looking at me, I don't care what the crowd thinks or says, I've come to touch Jesus and I'm not going to leave until I've done that very thing."

To touch Jesus takes an effort on your part, just as it took an effort on the part of the woman with the issue of blood.

Sometimes the blessings of God come in a service during the first song. I was preaching in California, and one night the song leader started singing, "There Is Power in the Blood." The Holy Ghost fell in that place, and by an hour later, five people had received the Holy Ghost.

But not every service begins like this. Sometimes the Lord says, "All right. If you want Me, if you really want to touch Me, you will have to seek Me." At such times what are you going to do? Sit back and watch things as a spectator, or try to reach out and touch Him?

You can touch God whether or not the preacher is your favorite, or whether or not you like the special singing, if He is there. And He said, "Where two or three are gathered together in my name, there am I in their midst." He's right in the middle of every meeting. He passes through every service. His garment is rippled by the winds of time, and all we have to do is reach out and touch Him with faith, and, thank God, His virtue will come into our bodies. Healing virtue, saving virtue, encouraging virtue. Nobody can stop God from blessing you if you really want a blessing.

Several years ago, I preached a revival in a church where there were several adults who needed the Holy Ghost. At the beginning of the revival, the pastor said to me, "Brother Willoughby, I have problems."

I asked, "What do you mean?"

He said, "These people who need the Holy Ghost are the type that only come to the altar about once every two or three months."

"Why do they come then?" I asked.

He replied, "If something unusual happens, if there is a message in tongues and interpretation, or if somebody falls under the power, they say, 'That's God,' and they'll come running to the altar and tell God they need the Holy Ghost. Then we may not see them again for three months."

I'm not against manifestations of the Spirit. I'm not against shouting. But if none of these things happen in a service, God is there anyway. We don't have to wait for these things. God is not always in the earthquake, the storm or the fire. Elijah had to learn that. Sometimes God speaks in a still, small voice. If you have faith in the Word of God, and believe that He is present, He will give you exactly what you need.

> *Reach out and touch the Lord as He passes by,*
> *You'll find He's not too busy to hear your heart's cry;*
> *He's passing by this moment, your needs to supply,*
> *Reach out and touch the Lord as He goes by.*

VALLEY OF DECISION

"Put ye in the sickle, for the harvest is ripe: come, get you down: for the press is full, the fats overflow; for their wickedness is great. Multitudes, multitudes in the valley of decision: for the day of the Lord is near in the valley of decision" (Joel 3:13, 14).

IN THIS message I want to talk, first of all, about decision making. What should I allow to influence me, and what should I not allow to influence me when it comes to making decisions, especially making decisions for God.

I also want to talk about the will of God. How many of you want to know the will of God? Want to do the will of God? We can't know too much about it; in fact, we all know too little about it. God help us to know more about His will.

We all have to make decisions. Some people are better at it than others, some are more responsible than others, some are more wise than others, yet, life is no respecter of persons, and we all have to make decisions. Poor people have to make them, just as rich people do. Meek people have to make them, just as bold people do. We make decisions every day.

Of course, most decisions you and I are called upon to make are quite light and easy to make, and, because of this, we make them without stopping to think, "Well, I'm making a decision." No, we just go ahead and do it.

For instance, when you are in revival and have church every night of the week, you are faced with a decision. "What dress am I going to wear tonight? What suit am I going to wear tonight?" When you go into a restaurant, and they hand you a menu, there are many things on it. The decision is yours. The waitress doesn't try to influence you in any way; she just stands there with a pad and pencil, waiting for you. There you are, pages full, and the decision is yours.

This is life. There are always decisions. When you walk to the breakfast table, what is it going to be? Bacon and eggs, oatmeal or cold Post Toasties?

Not all decisions are small, though; sometimes they are big, sometimes they involve a lot of money. Sometimes they involve where we are going to live, our jobs or our professions. Maybe some of you will be graduating from high school before very long. You are faced with a decision, "Am I going to go to college? If I am going to college, which one is it going to be?" Life is like the links in a chain: making one decision just leads to having to make another one.

No doubt someone is driving a car that is getting old. Things are starting to go wrong with it, it's getting miles on it. It won't be long before you will be faced with a decision. What are you going to do with it? Trade it in on another used one or trade it in on a new one? If you trade it in on a new one, what is it going to be? Ford? Plymouth? Chevrolet? Then when you decide what car you are after, there is that other decision. What kind of options do you want? What color do you want? When you decide all of that, still you have another decision to make: How are you going to pay for it?

Some decisions involve not only money but they involve which church you attend. Where you live will determine the companionship you have. Whether you are close to mom or away from mom, close to the family or away from the family. These are decisions that involve people, places and money.

I want to emphasize the importance of making decisions for the Lord, and making them rightly, properly and righteously, because the salvation of your soul depends on it. Your soul salvation will not depend upon what you had for breakfast this morning. It doesn't make a bit of difference whether you had scrambled eggs and bacon, or oatmeal. I don't care what kind of car you may be driving; it could be a Ford or a Cadillac. Your soul salvation won't depend on making decisions like that.

But every once-in-a-while we come to a place in our lives that Joel calls, "The valley of decision." That is the valley of all valleys. Somewhere down life's road we all have to step into it. When you step into that valley, you are faced with making a decision about the Lord.

There are some things that you should not allow to influence you when you are trying to make a decision for God, and if you do allow those things to influence you, it will destroy your judgment. That's right! Then your soul will be lost and your destiny will be the lake of fire.

There are, basically, three things that you should not allow to influence you when you are faced with making a decision that involves the will of the Lord.

First, don't let your relatives influence you. When the call of God is on your life, and you are in the valley of decision, you are there all by yourself. You had better forget you even have a mother or father. You had better forget you even have a brother or a sister. When God speaks to you and calls you, He calls you as an individual. People don't come to God on a family plan. People who come to God, come on an individual basis.

Jesus said, "Suppose ye that I am come to give peace on earth? I tell you, Nay; but rather division. The father shall be divided against the son, and the son against the father; the mother against the daughter, and the daugh-

ter against the mother; the mother-in-law against her
daughter-in-law, and the daughter-in-law against her
mother-in-law" (Luke 12:51, 53). That is the way it is in
the kingdom of God. There is a division, even in families.
Jesus said, "If any man love mother or father, son or
daughter more than me, he is not worthy of me." That is
one of the prerequisites for walking with God, with
counting the cost. You must be willing to pay the price
of putting God ahead of your relatives.

"Seek ye first the kingdom of God, . . . and all these
other things shall be added unto you." God will take care
of those things. You cannot walk with God, you cannot
successfully live for God if you are putting your family
ahead of Him. Believe it or not, that is one of the biggest
things that stops people from living for God today.

That was one of the excuses Jesus talked about in the
Bible when the call of God came, inviting people to a
great supper. One man said, "I have married a wife, and
I cannot come." Family relationship should never come
before the call of God.

Someone said, "Well, don't you know that blood is
thicker than water?" Yes, I know blood is thicker than
water, but I'll tell you something else that you'll find
equally as true: When you are baptized in Jesus' name
and filled with the Holy Ghost, the Spirit is thicker than
blood. When you are born again, you'll feel a closer
relationship with the household of God than you do your
own relations.

One of the biggest things that stops people from really
giving their hearts to God is the reaction of their relatives. When you try to walk with God you have a fight
on your hands. That's when the Devil will try to bring
your relatives into it.

I talked to a man one time, and he was typical of so

many today. He was a Campbellite. I talked to him about the importance of baptism in Jesus' name and the in-filling of the Holy Ghost. He took the attitude, "Well, I don't believe you have to be baptized that way. I don't believe you have to have the Holy Ghost, because my mother wasn't baptized in Jesus' name, she didn't have the Holy Ghost, and when she was on her deathbed she saw the angels of God coming to get her. You'll never make me believe that my good old mom didn't go to heaven."

If you're using that kind of attitude as a basis for your walk with God, you are in error. It is an error to use your dead relative as a criterion for your walk with God instead of using the Word of God. When you are in the valley of decision, it doesn't make any difference what dear old grandma did or did not do. Your relatives are going to stand before God. I can't put them in heaven or hell, and you can't either. If they go to heaven, it will be God that takes them there, and if they go to hell it will be God that commands them to go there. They will go to one of the two places, depending on whether or not they obeyed the Word of the Lord.

The same thing applies to us. Either we take the broad road that leads to destruction, or we take the straight and narrow way that leads into life everlasting. It depends on whether we mold our lives to fit the Bible or try to alter the Bible to fit our lives, or to suit our philosophy.

Relatives stop many people from coming to God. Many women do not attend church because their husbands object. There are a lot of husbands who could attend but do not, because of their wives. The same is true of parents and their children.

When you are in the valley of decision, and faced with making a decision for God, it is between you and the

Lord, and it must be a personal, individual matter. Don't let your relatives influence you.

Rebekah was a good example. Abraham sent his servant, Eliezer, back to the land of Nahor to get a bride for his son Isaac. When that servant came to the well and put out his "fleece," God heard and answered it before he hardly got the words out of his mouth. Here came Rebekah with the water pitcher and she offered to draw water for him and for all the camels. Eliezer raised his hands and worshipped God for answering his prayer.

He went to her father's house, and put the question to them. He said, "All right, I'm going to tell you why I've come. My master, Abraham, has a son who, at the age of forty, is still an eligible bachelor. Abraham believes, firmly, that God has provided from among your people a bride, and I believe it is Rebekah. So they all gathered around: mom, dad, sisters and brothers, and put the question to her point-blank. "Will you go with this man?"

Think of the magnitude of that decision. Would you, as a young girl, have done it? Would you have left mother, father, brother, sister? Would you have left your native country? Would you have left the old familar streets and lanes and sights? Would you have left your chums, the ones you were brought up with? Would you have left all that and have gone with a total, absolute stranger whom you had never laid eyes on before? That is the kind of decision she was called upon to make.

I like her courage, her faith. She jumped up and said, "I will go." She loved her mom and dad, but she left Mesopotamia, the land she was reared in. She left it all to go with this stranger, and journeyed with him on a camel.

Because of her decision, because of her spiritual foresight, because of her great faith in God, and because she took a journey by faith, she ended up being married to a man of faith. Pilgrim married pilgrim. Isaac and Rebekah were united in marriage, and she turned out to be a wife of one of the greatest patriarchs who ever lived. This brought her into the direct blood line of the Messiah.

The Holy Ghost is God's agent, moving in the affairs of men. When He first knocked on your door, he knocked as a stranger. Maybe you had never met Him, but here is the question He asked, "Are you willing to give up your sinful friends? If necessary, are you willing to leave mom and dad? Are you willing to give up the dance hall? Are you willing to give up the glitter and glamor of this world? Are you willing to take a journey of faith? Are you willing to go on a journey with Me?"

Oh, I'm so glad that about twelve years ago that gentle Stranger came knocking on my heart's door. It was none other than the wooing of the Holy Ghost. I walked down the aisle to an altar, and said, "Yes, I'll go, I'll take that journey of faith."

The Holy Ghost is preparing a bride, the Holy Ghost is getting the bride ready, the Holy Ghost is taking us on our way. Just as Rebekah, we were aliens, we were not born Jews. But we have been adopted into the family because we said an eternal, "Yes," to the Holy Ghost.

Ruth was another good example. If you want to read a beautiful chapter, read Ruth, chapter one. It tells about a woman, Naomi, who took a journey to Moab. Her husband died, then her two sons, who had married Moabite girls, died.

Naomi said, "The hand of God is gone out against me; I'm going back to Bethlehem." So she called her daughters-in-law, Orpah and Ruth, and said, "God's hand has gone out against me. I'm a widow now, and both of you are

widows. Surely you are not going to wait for me to re-
marry and raise sons for you to marry. Go back, my
daughters, go back to your homes, go back to your
people. Go back to your old familiar haunts. Go back."

They both had to make their decisions. Orpah kissed
Naomi, and went back. But we don't read that Ruth
kissed Naomi; we do read that she clave unto her. And
these are the words that she said to her: "Entreat me not
to leave thee, . . . for whither thou goest, I will go. And
where thou lodgest, I will lodge: thy people shall be my
people, and thy God shall be my God." She had made her
decision.

"I'm going to leave, Mom. I'm going to say goodbye,
Dad. I may never see you again as long as I live. The
kids I was raised with, the old familiar haunts, the old
familiar places we visited — I may never see them again,
but I'm saying goodbye to them all, right now; I'm going
with this woman of God. She has made her decision, so
I've made mine. I'm going to cleave unto her."

Because of her decision, God saw something in that
woman. She was a Moabite, and Moabites were descen-
dants of Lot. They were illegitimate children, and they
were looked upon by the Hebrews as heathen. Yet, when
Naomi brought this woman back to Israel, everybody
noticed that she was a woman of gravity, a woman of
sincerity.

Ruth finally married Boaz, the kinsman redeemer.
They had a son whose name was Obed, he had a son
whose name was Jessie, and he had a son whose name
was David. There you have another example of how just
an out-and-out Gentile, an outsider, a woman from a
heathen nation decided to put God first, and God called
her to be in the direct blood line of the Messiah. She was
the great-grandmother of David, who was the forefather

of Jesus Christ.

It is a wonderful thing when the call of God is on your life as an individual, and when you respond to that call. That, and that alone, will bring you into the kingdom of God. It will make you a child of the king. His royal blood will flow through your veins.

The call of God is not just for the Hebrews or Jews, but it is for all those that are afar off, even as many as the Lord our God shall call.

Don't let friends influence you. Proverbs 1:10 says, "My son, if sinners entice thee, consent thou not." You know, a lot of souls are destroyed because of wrong companionship. Young people, if you start running with the wrong people and the wrong companions, you may lose your soul. The old expression is true: A man is known by the company he keeps. Who you run with will reveal where your heart is.

Where you spend your time will also show where your heart is. If you spend all your time around sinners, that is where your heart is. If you spend all your time at places of worldly pleasure, that is where your heart is. But if you devote your time to Bible study and prayer, and working for God, and helping the people of God, then that is where your heart is. Don't let friends wrongly influence you.

Don't let appearance influence you. John 7:24 says, "Judge not according to the appearance, but judge righteous judgment." You can't judge by appearance. How do I know? Because the Bible says, "There is a way that seemeth right unto a man, but the end thereof are the ways of death."

You can't judge something by looking at it on the surface. Some things look right. The Zodiac looks right, the horoscope looks right. It looks as if it is hitting right

on the mark, but the Bible bears out that it is a dead-end
street. It is not for God's people to indulge in. I don't
believe that God's people should resort to spiritualism
and witchcraft, or turn to wizards. If we read the handwriting on the wall, it is because God helps us to see it.
It is because we have confidence in a man of God somewhere that can interpret it for us. We don't want to run
to the crystal ball gazers of this world, but we want to
keep our confidence in the Lord.

If we are going to let anything influence us in making
decisions for God, let it be either one of two things, or
both.

First, let it be the Spirit of God. Romans 8:14 says, "For
as many as are led by the Spirit of God, they are the sons
of God." When God speaks to us, we should obey that still
small, voice. Friend, it is a voice that influences.

Secondly, we should obey the **Word** of God. The Word
of the Lord is forever settled in heaven, and, further-
more, it is a lamp unto our feet and a light unto our
pathway. It can show us the next step we ought to take,
and, at the same time, it can show us the general trend
and pathway that lies ahead.

God's Word can help us make decisions for the Lord.
God's Word still has the answers to many of our questions. God's roadmap, God's blueprint for eternity — it is
all wrapped up in the Word of God.

Spirit and truth: those are the two things we should
allow to influence us, and the good thing about it is that
they never conflict. They never fight against one another.
When God reveals the truth through the Word and
through His Spirit, it is going to harmonize.

God deals with different people in different ways. How
many of you have ever received a dream from God? How
many of you have ever had a vision from God? A dream

is at night, a vision is when you are conscious and awake; that's how we define the difference between the two.

Have you ever heard the audible voice of God? Have you ever seen an angel? I believe in the appearance of angels. I believe in dreams, and I believe in visions. In fact, the Bible says that in the last days young men will see visions, and old men will dream dreams. God is moving.

But every time there is a dream or a vision or an audible voice, or even an angel appearing unto you with a message, it will harmonize with God's Word.

They that worship God must worship Him in Spirit and in truth. He gives the Spirit and He gives the truth. It all comes from God, and it all works together. They are geared in the same piece of machinery, helping us to find the will of God for our lives in order to be saved in the end. Isn't that beautiful?

Someone may ask, "How can I know the will of God, how can I **really** know the will of God for my life?

Some people spend their whole lives thinking that the will of God is something totally mystic, something that is absolutely and completely beyond reach. But the will of God is found in the Bible. The good old King James Version is a whole book full of God's will. God's will doesn't have to be spoken out loud. It can be written down on paper.

There are some things we don't have to pray about, because God has already revealed them in the Bible. For instance, I've had some young person come to me and say, "Brother Willoughby, pray for me; I've been dating a sinner, and I'm going to be a missionary, so I want you to help me pray about it. I want the will of God in this matter."

Do you know what I tell this person? I say, "I'm not

going to pray five seconds for you. You already have your answer. Why pray about something that's already answered?" 2 Corinthians 6:14 says, "Be ye not unequally yoked together with unbelievers: for what fellowship hath righteousness with unrighteousness? and what communion hath light with darkness?" If you think that it is the will of God for saints to marry sinners, you are sadly mistaken. That is the doctrine of Balaam. God regards it as an abomination. He said, "Come out from among them, and be ye separate."

I've had people come to me and say, "Brother Willoughby, pray for me. I've been thinking about starting to pay my tithes. God has been dealing with me."

I say, "Listen, I'm not going to pray for you. You already know God's will. Tithe paying was commanded before there ever was a Law. It was under the Law, it was after the Law. It was before Pentecost, it was after Pentecost, and it is even today. It belongs to God."

"Brother Willoughby, pray for me. I've been thinking about attending the mid-week Bible study, instead of going out and doing something else. Pray for me. God has been dealing with me rather strongly about it."

Don't ask me to help you pray, don't ask me to join you in prayer about that. You already have your answer: "Not forsaking the assembling of ourselves together. . . ." (Hebrews 10:25). If there is any service we ought to be in, it is a good Bible study service. I like Bible study. If you don't, something is wrong with you. You can't be a Christian and not love God's Word.

All this reminds me of the story about a man and his wife who were making a decision concerning moving to Phoenix, Arizona. "Honey," he said, "I really want you to get down in earnest with God about this matter. I want you to go into that living room and get in earnest with

God. I want you to really get hold of the Lord, and find His will. While you're praying, I'll be packing."

That's not giving God a chance. "Now Lord, You can say, 'Yes' or you can say, 'No,' but as far as I'm concerned, it's 'Yes.'" That's the way a lot of people are today. They come to church and they say, "All right, you can preach anything you want to, but no matter what you preach, I'm going to keep my barriers, my traditions, I'm still going to keep my own ideas. You preach anything you want to, but I'm going to close my eyes and turn you off." It's like listening to a preacher on the radio. If he gets to stepping on your toes, or if he starts coming right down your line, all you have to do is turn that knob a little bit, and zip, there he goes down the road.

There are at least two prerequisites to knowing the will of God. One is that you must surrender your will, for as long as **your** will is in the way, you can never know **His** will. There are two wills involved. Even in the life of Jesus Christ, this was true. Jesus said, "I seek not mine own will, but the will of the Father which hath sent me" (John 5:30). He had a will of His own, separate from the will of God. That's why there had to be a Gethsemane. That's where the surrender was made. He said, "Not my will but thine be done." And if we ever expect to know the will of God, to do the will of God, we must have a Gethsemane in our own lives. The Lord will never impose His will on our wills. Our wills have to be broken and out of the way before God will bring His into the picture.

An example of this was when Jesus cast all the devils out of the demoniac of Gadara. He commanded them to go into a herd of swine, which then ran violently down a steep place into the water and were drowned. The townspeople came and said, "Leave! We don't want anything to do with you." They were troubled and angry.

The same Jesus who had the power to cast those devils out, the same Jesus who could cause that man to be sitting clothed, and in his right mind, also had the power to stay there if He had wanted to stay. But here is proof that God does not force His will, does not superimpose His will. The same Jesus who had power to stay, quietly turned around and left.

If you don't want God's will, then you won't have it. You have to want it.

Our wills have to be broken before God's will can be done. There is a blessing in brokenness.

A lad came unto Jesus, and all he had was five loaves and two fishes — a little lunch. But Jesus took it, broke it, blessed it, gave it to His disciples, and the disciples gave it to the crowd. They fed between five and ten thousand people. After they ate until they were filled, they picked up twelve baskets full. But the bread and fish had to be broken before it could be blessed.

The woman who came to Jesus with the precious ointment did not pour out the ointment and keep the box. The Bible says she broke the box. This was a final act of consecration. The sweet fragrance filled the room. Why? Because she had broken the alabaster box. It was broken to bless.

Then at the Communion table, Jesus said, "Take, eat: this is my body, which is broken for you." Did you know that Jesus Himself couldn't bless us until He was broken? Did you know that as long as He was in perfect health, He couldn't bless you and me? He opened blinded eyes, He unstopped deaf ears, He restored withered arms, He cleansed lepers, He even raised the dead, but that wasn't doing you and me any good. As long as He had a healthy, strong body, He couldn't reach out across the Atlantic Ocean. His blessings were just local.

There came a time when they led Him to a whipping post, took a cat-o'-nine-tails and laid stripes on His back. That was when He started to be broken, then He could start to bless everybody. When they laid those stripes on His back, there went your heart trouble, there went your crutches, there went your broken bones, there went your muscular dystrophy, there went your spinal meningitis, there went your cancer. What happened? His being broken was making it possible for us to be blessed.

Then they led Him to Calvary, drove nails through His hands and feet and put a spear through His side. It was awful, the torture, the sacrifice and suffering that was involved. But there went your cigarettes, there went your alcohol, there went your dope addiction. Today, He may not be turning water into wine, but He is turning "whiskey into groceries," He is changing sinners into new creatures, making them new individuals. When He was broken at Calvary, that was when His blood began to reach into other cities and towns. You and I are living proof that Calvary has reached us today.

They tell me that one of the most famous horse ranches in all the world is down by Corpus Christi, Texas, and is called the King's Ranch. That ranch trains all kinds of horses: show horses, race horses, and others. But no matter what kind of horse they are dealing with, what is the first thing on the schedule? Is it to teach it to stop? No. To teach it to turn right? No. The first thing on the schedule, no matter what kind of horse it is, is to break the spirit of that horse. If that can't be accomplished, then nothing else can even be started. We are on the **"King's** ranch." I want you to know that God will never put a bit and a bridle on us, we will never be able to receive signals from Him saying, "Go, stop, turn left, turn right," until, first of all, our spirits are broken and out of the way.

God can't do anything with you, God can't even speak to you, get through to you until, first of all, you are willing to yield and submit. To commit yourself to Calvary and to yield yourself to the message of the truth. It is wonderful when we get our wills subdued, and His will is done. There is nothing more wonderful than doing the will of God.

Multitudes, multitudes, in the valley of decision. If you are feeling the tug of God at your heart, the call of God on your soul, don't turn Him away as you have done so many times. If you are not feeling right toward God and the church, you can yield to Him, and have a lot more love toward God, a love toward the man of God, a love toward the Word of God, and a love toward the people of God.

The day of the Lord is near in the valley of decision.

You cannot do God's will, so long as your will is in the way. You have to get to the place where you are yielded, and say, "All right, God, it is not my will that I want, it is not my way that I want. Lord, whatever You will, whatever is written in the Book, I want to do it. If the book says to be baptized in Jesus' name, then I want to do it. Lord, if it says to receive the Holy Ghost, with speaking in tongues, I want to do it. Lord, if it says to live for You, to serve You and be faithful, then Lord, I want to do it. If it says to honor the ministry and to back the man of God, then Lord, I want to do it. Not my will, but thine be done."

If you will develop that kind of attitude, just as Rebekah and Ruth did, you'll find yourself in the family of God, in the family of the King, a royal priesthood and a holy nation of a peculiar people who have been called out of darkness into marvelous light.

NOT FOR SALE

"And it came to pass after these things, that Naboth the Jezreelite had a vineyard, which was in Jezreel, hard by the palace of Ahab king of Samaria. And Ahab spake unto Naboth, saying, Give me thy vineyard, that I may have it for a garden of herbs, because it is near unto my house: and I will give thee for it a better vineyard than it; or, if it seem good to thee, I will give thee the worth of it in money" (1 Kings 21:1, 2).

I AM GOING to begin by bringing to your remembrance the story of Esau and Jacob. Esau was the firstborn. Jacob had to settle with being the second born. By that I mean that there were certain blessings for the firstborn. It was the Hebrew custom that the right hand would be laid upon the eldest son, and that the birthright automatically belonged to him.

What was the birthright? It was what people today would call the inheritance. It involved the covenant that God had orginally made with Abraham. It was a carry-over of this covenant. So the birthright included not only money, cattle, and herds; it also involved being in the lineage of the Messiah. There was a spiritual aspect to it.

Abraham had given it to Isaac. Ishmael was the firstborn, but he was not born of Sarah, the free woman, but was of the bond woman. That disqualified him. The eldest son, born of a free woman, was the one who got the birthright. Isaac had the birthright, and, in like manner, so did Esau. The birthright made them the priest of the family. It made them the spiritual head. God said, "I will bless them that bless you and curse them that curse you."

Esau, even though he had the birthright, didn't respect it. He didn't regard it, he didn't appreciate it.

What was the difference between Esau and Jacob? They had the same mom and dad, they were born about the same time, and brought up in the same family. They had equal opportunity, and yet they were different. One of them was spiritually minded, the other was carnally minded. One of them was indifferent to the things of God, the other desired the things of God. That was the difference between Esau and Jacob.

Esau was a man of the field, a hunter. His hair was red. He was earthly, not only in his physical appearance, but in the very attitude he manifested.

Jacob was different. The Bible says that he was a dweller in the tents. He was a favorite of his mother, Rebekah. He stayed close to home. He was the steward of the household. Instead of spending all the day running around, he loved to stay at home to keep the books and tend to the sheep; to nourish the young ones in a gentle way. This was Jacob.

Two boys! Brothers? Yes. Same ancestry? Yes. Same home? Yes. Yet there was as much difference in those boys as night and day.

Esau had a lot of things going for him. He was physically strong. He was a great hunter, and he fixed venison for his father just the way old Isaac liked it. Still, he was a man who had no respect for the things of God. He would hear things in one ear, and they would go right out the other. He wasn't listening to those stories of faith that grandpa Abraham and father Isaac had told him and his brother.

But Jacob was listening. When he grew up it was almost a part of him. He longed to receive the blessing of God. He looked for an opportunity to get the favor of

God, to get the birthright, and to get the right hand of blessing laid on his head. He craved those things.

David said, "As the hart panteth after the water brooks, so panteth my soul after thee, O God." A lot of people in the world today have no respect for God. They have no craving for God. It is a beautiful thing when somebody in this world has a spiritual appetite instead of only a physical appetite.

While Esau was looking at the beans, Jacob was looking at the birthright. That was the difference in the two. One had an eye that was viewing the world, the other had an eye that was viewing spiritual and heavenly possibilities.

One day the opportunity came, the chance of a lifetime came. Esau had been out trying to find a deer. He had had a bad day, you know. Have you had days like that? You know, when everything goes wrong, everything goes backwards. You feel like asking, "Why don't I just go back to bed and forget it?" Well, Esau was a skillful, cunning hunter, but that day he didn't kill a deer. He had no meat.

He came dragging in about the time that Jacob was stirring up some bean soup, pea soup, or something of that order. The Bible says that it was savoury. Mmm-mmmm! Good! Perhaps it would have put Campbells out of business.

Esau came in, and the first thing he thought of was God? No! The first thing he thought of was his stomach. You see, that's old Esau. Isn't that a picture of him? He said, "Give me some of that red pottage, some of that pottage with lentiles so that I may live and not die. I am at the point of death."

Jacob saw a real opportunity. You know, a real Jew will always look for a bargain. They know a good deal when they see it, and Jacob was no exception to the rule. This was the day he'd been looking for. He jumped up and said, "All right, I'll give you some of this if you'll sell me your birthright. Come on, let's just make a quick exchange; I'll give you a bowl of soup and you give me your birthright."

Would you believe it? It is strange and ironical that Esau gave him the birthright for a bowl of soup. That doesn't make sense, but it is in the Bible.

I'm glad they put that story in the Bible. Do you know why? Because it is so typical of what people today are doing. There are people who will sell their birthright for a bowl of soup. These are people who take the treasures of God and play with them like they were trifles. That's right! They are childish about the things of the Lord, indifferent to them, and very disrespectful toward them.

Esau was like this. He actually sold the birthright. And along with it there went the headship of the family, there went the priesthood of the family, there went the covenant blessings of Abraham, there went all hope of ever being the ancestor of the Messiah, the promised Redeemer. He traded all that for a bowl of soup and a piece of bread. He sold out! The Bible says he went away, and thus despised his birthright.

Later, he came with tears on his cheeks, kneeling down before his father, saying, "Father, don't I get a blessing too?" The Bible says that he sought repentance carefully, with tears.

Doesn't God honor repentance? Doesn't God honor tears? Yes, if they are in time. But there is such a thing as a time factor. You can wait too late, procrastinate, and put it off too long, for God said, "My Spirit will not always strive." There will come a time when there will be tears, there will be repentance and there will be people crying at the altars, but God won't hear it.

One day after the rapture, the churches will be packed out. You talk about a revival that will stop the ball games. This is going to happen, but it will be too late when it does happen. There is going to be a revival one of these days that will close all the poolhalls. Where are the people going to be? They're going to be outside, screaming, pulling their hair, saying, "Well, the preacher told us." But it's going to be too late. The church is going to be gone.

Going back to Esau, he sold his birthright and then he tried to get it back, but it was too late. The Bible gives us several illustrations of people who, like Esau, sold out on something precious from God.

Judas was one. He walked with the Lord just as Andrew did, as John did, as Philip did, as Simon Peter did. He saw the same things they saw, heard the same things they heard, and went to many of the same places they went to. Yes, Judas followed the Lord. He saw the multitude fed, he saw the blind eyes opened, he saw deaf ears unstopped.

There was Judas, handpicked by the Lord to carry the moneybag, who saw the miracles that God had given them. But apparently it did not affect him. He went unto the high priest and, in a subtle way, in a deceptive way, made plans to betray Jesus for thirty pieces of silver. He sold out the very One who had worked all of those miracles. His life had not been affected by what he had seen, or by what he had heard. He was like Esau. What he heard just went in one ear and right out the other.

The Bible says, "He that hath an ear, let him hear what the Spirit saith." We ought to have ears that are in tune with heaven, not the kind of ears that don't let the Word of God affect us. It ought to affect us, it ought to wake us up. If God's Word won't do it, what will?

Judas, like Esau, sold out. And like Esau, he also repented. The Bible says in Matthew 27:3 that Judas repented. Did God honor it? No.

This proves that there is such a thing as going beyond the limits of the call of God. There is such a thing as going beyond the point of no return, where you are beyond the mercy of God, until God doesn't even deal with you anymore. You are beyond the reach of God's love, you are forever lost, even though you are living.

Judas repented, not only in word but also in deed. He took every bit of that silver back, threw it down at the priests' feet, and said, "I don't want it. I have betrayed innocent blood." Then he went out, filled with remorse about it all, and hanged himself.

There was another man whose name had been written in the Lambs' book of life. He was a comrade of the Apostle Paul, one of the greatest men who ever lived, the apostle to the Gentiles, a man full of the presence of God. This man's name was Demas. For awhile he was faithful, but in one Epistle Paul said, "Demas hath forsaken me, having loved this present world." Just as Esau, and just as Judas, Demas sold out the blessings of God.

If you think the Hebrews had a birthright, the New Testament Christians had a birthright greater than any that Esau and Jacob ever dreamed about. The New Testament birthright involves redemption, justification, sanctification, the gifts of the Spirit, along with joy unspeakable and full of glory. This could go on and on, for there is also divine healing, and the blessings of God that come along with the infilling of the Holy Ghost.

Demas traded every bit of that for the few little pleasures of the city of Thessalonica. He said, "I want to go out there and enjoy the pleasures that are on the streets of the city." And he did. He turned his back on the Lord, and rejected salvation and the call of God. What a tragedy! We have no record of his ever getting back to God. We have no record of his ever being reinstated, and his name being put back into the Lamb's book of life.

People who backslide take such a chance. Some people play with God as if He were a toy. He is not! Salvation is a serious thing. It is a matter of life and death. It is God's will that we get in, and do our very best to stay in. How? By the miracle of love and grace. If we stand, if we are successful at all, it will be because of the grace of God. His grace is sufficient for you, His grace is sufficient for me. We don't need anything else to help us live for God other than His grace, the help and strength of God.

Esau sold out, so did Judas, so did Demas.

My original text introduced us to a man by the name of Naboth. He is an example for all of us. He isn't preached about very often, but he is in there. His life story doesn't take up very many verses, but I thank God for the testimony of him. He owned a vineyard that was near the palace in Jezreel, and Ahab the king wanted that vineyard. Ahab went unto him and said, "Naboth, sell me your vineyard. I'll give you the price in money, or if that doesn't suit you, I'll give you a vineyard that is better. Sell it to me. I'd like to have it for a garden of herbs."

Naboth looked at Ahab and said, "It is not for sale."

Ahab shook his head, "Why? I can't see what is the matter. Why don't you want to sell it to me? All you have is just a few little fig trees and a few little grape vines; there's not much to it at all. Why won't you sell it to me?"

But Naboth answered, "You don't understand. You only see fig trees, you only see grape vines. I want you to know I see more than that. This is the inheritance of my father. It is not for sale."

Ahab tried and tried to get Naboth to give in, but he would not. Ahab was enraged, and went back to his palace, pouting, just like a little boy. He jumped into bed and put his face to the wall.

Jezebel, the real brains behind the operation, the wicked queen, came in and said, "What are you pouting about? Why are you feeling so bad?

Ahab said, "Naboth wouldn't sell me his vineyard." He was pouting like a little child whose toys had been taken away from him.

She said, "Well, you're the king. Why don't you do something about it? Let me take care of it."

She was a bold, brazen, cruel woman. She had letters written, with Ahab's signature, and they sent them to the city of Jezreel. Then false accusers and false witnesses put Naboth in a place of judgment. They witnessed against him, and said that he had spoken blasphemy against the king and against the nation. Then they took him outside the gates of the city and stoned him to death.

While they were stoning him to death, the same vineyard that he had in his possession earlier, was still in his possession. The same vineyard that he held in life, he still held in death.

The Lord said, "Be thou faithful unto death and I will give thee a crown of life." Jezebel is a type of the Devil, and the Devil is using his "Ahab" to try to make us give up our vineyards. But it is the inheritance of the Father. There is more to Pentecost than just singing in the choir. There is more to Pentecost than just playing a musical instrument. There is more to Pentecost than being able to quote scriptures. We are heirs with God, and joint heirs with Jesus Christ.

When you sell out to the Devil, you're giving away

more than a million, quadrillion dollars. You need to put up a sign, "Not for sale." Your car might have a price tag on it. But you need to learn, as you journey through life, that some things come into your possession that are so precious they should never have a price tag.

One of those things is the call of God, and our walk with Him. Ahab looked at that vineyard and saw only a few fig trees and a few small grape vines. By the same token, people are trying to get us to sell out. All they can see is our going to church, going to church, going to church. They say, "You're always going through the same old ritual, the same old ceremony."

There is a difference, however, in standing on the outside looking in and standing on the inside looking out. When the Tabernacle was set up, all you could see on the outside was badger skins, and goat and rams' skins dyed red. In other words, it had the appearance of being dull and dark. But on the inside there were not rams' skins dyed red, there was a golden candlestick, there was silver and brass, there was a table of shew bread, there was the altar of incense, there was the Ark of the Covenant and the Mercy Seat, on which was sprinkled the blood of a lamb.

When the flood came in the days of Noah, you would have thanked God if you were on the inside of the ark looking out, and not on the outside looking in.

What does your vineyard mean to you? For a few minutes, think of your vineyard as your church. You will think only as much of your church as it directly relates to the experiences you have received from God in that church.

If you are carnal, like Esau, never co-operating, never worshipping God, never calling upon the name of the Lord, never letting your soul get blessed, never speaking in other tongues, never letting the joy of the Lord reign in your soul, never weeping before the Lord, never shouting, you don't have anything to sell.

But if God has really given you a spiritual inheritance, and has brought you into kinship with the Messiah by adopting you into the family of God; if He has sent that joy and that peace, the peace that passeth all understanding, then you feel yourself drawing water out of the well of salvation with joy.

When the Devil comes around trying to allure you and attract you with the "Ahabs" of this world, trying to get you to sell out, that's when you need to put up the sign, "Not for Sale." You should say, "I'm going to live for God, I'm going to serve the Lord, I'm going to be faithful to the end, for if I'm faithful to Him, He'll be faithful to me. If I draw nigh unto Him, He'll draw nigh unto me. If I give my best to Him, He'll give His best to me."

Once you are really rooted and grounded in the church, you won't have any desire whatsoever to backslide. You ought to think a lot of your church and your pastor. You ought to think a lot of your God and His Word. When you sell out on God, those are the things you are giving away, maybe never to be placed in your hands again.

We need the spirit that Moses had. "By faith Moses . . . refused to be called the son of Pharaoh's daughter; choosing rather to suffer affliction with the people of God. . . ." Why? Because he had respect unto the recompense of the reward.

God doesn't always pay off at the first of the month. Some people are impatient. They sacrifice their tomorrow's on the altar of today. They want their pleasures now, they want worldly lusts now, they want physical fulfillments now, they want carnal blessings now. They are not willing to wait for God's real blessings. So, therefore, they sell out for just a few little carnal pleasures. That is what Esau did.

If you do anything at all, hold on to God. What you have in Christ Jesus is worth more than silver and gold. It's not for sale.

In the eighth chapter of Acts, Simon the sorcerer "got his wallet out," and said, "I've got some money I want to give. In return, I'd like to have power to give people the Holy Ghost."

You know what Simon Peter told Simon the sorcerer? "Put your wallet away, forget it; your money perish with you because you even thought that the gift of God could be purchased with money. I perceive that you are in the gall of bitterness and the bond of iniquity. I pray that God will forgive you for the thoughts of your heart."

It is sinful even to think that you can put a price tag on the blessings of God. When you are baptized in Jesus' name, your sins are remitted and you are filled with the Holy Ghost. You have joy unspeakable. No amount of money, not all the gold in Ft. Knox nor all the glitter and glamor of this world, can be compared with what you have.

There was a man known as "Stocky." He was a good football and baseball player. In spite of his stocky build, he was able to run the one hundred yard dash in ten seconds flat. This young man had a $20,000 baseball contract pending with the Pittsburg Pirates. But he turned it down and went to Bible college. He is now pastoring a little home missions work in the Illinois District. Is he discouraged, is he despondent about the whole business? Is he sorry that he lost $20,000 and gave up a profession, and fame and fortune? Instead, he is pastoring a work that isn't even big enough to support him, and he has to work and run a milk route. Is he sorry? No, he is one of the most jolly young men I have ever met. He's full of life, he's happy. Why? Because he's in the kingdom; he's still got his vineyard.

Ahab said, "I want your vineyard."

Naboth said, "No, no, no! I'm happy with my vineyard."

I'm glad for our Pentecostal heritage. I'm glad for such men as W. T. Witherspoon, S. L. Wise, A. T. Morgan, and for all the men who devoted their lives getting this message to you and me. That is part of the inheritance. Let us not sell out.

I went to Bible School with a boy who gave up $25,000 he could have had if he had pitched for the St. Louis Cardinals. He turned it down, and accepted the pastorate of a church. It is now a very large, thriving church. This young man is being blessed of God, being used of God as a spiritual leader in the vineyard.

What do you want for the vineyard? No deal, no trade, not for sale! Sometimes people take the precious gift of God, what God has given them, to the bargain table of this old world. But I'm going to hold on to it. I'm going to cleave to it.

The Lord spoke to the church of Philadelphia and said, "Hold fast that which you have that no man take your crown." No amount of fame, no amount of fortune, no amount of money ought to make us willing to trade.

The Devil has offered everything that's got a name, all the wealth I want, and the fame of this old world, but listen, Devil, I wouldn't take nothing for my journey now. I've got to make it to heaven somehow. I can see the light of the lighthouse. We're going around the last turn, we're on the home stretch, headed for the finish line. We're headed for that city where the Lamb is the light.

Your experience and my experience — it is not for sale. It is a gift from the heavenly Father. It is not for sale at any price.

When the Devil comes around, you can put the sign out that says, "Not for Sale." And he'll say, "Why?" Then you'll begin to sing,

> *Precious memories, how they linger,*
> *How they ever flood my soul;*
> *In the stillness of the midnight,*
> *Precious sacred scenes unfold.*

I remember when I spoke in tongues. I remember when my sins were remitted. I remember shouting down the aisle, and laughing in the Spirit. Precious memories — how they flood my soul.

But the church should mean more than this to you. It should mean the study of the Word of God. Your vineyard ought to mean more to you than just a song, more than just the raising of the hand or lifting of the voice. There is more to Pentecost than just ritual and ceremony and traditions. Behind it all, or rather underneath it all are the everlasting arms of God. In His presence is fulness of joy; at His right hand are pleasures for evermore. "The kingdom of God is not meat and drink but righteousness, peace and joy in the Holy Ghost."

We are in the same kingdom that many grandmas and grandpas shouted in. This is a kingdom that moms and dads shouted in; aunts and uncles. It is the inheritance of the fathers. You and I can shout in it. You speak with tongues just as Andrew and John spoke, just as Simon Peter and the Apostle Paul spoke.

This is our inheritance. *And it is not for sale.*

GOD'S ABIDING PRESENCE

Therefore sent he thither horses, and chariots, and a great host: and they came by night and compassed the city about. And when the servant of the man of God was risen early, and gone forth, behold, an host compassed the city both with horses and chariots. And his servant said unto him, Alas my master! how shall we do? And he answered, Fear not: for they that be with us are more than they that be with them. And Elisha prayed, and said, Lord, I pray thee, open his eyes, that he may see. And the Lord opened the eyes of the young man; and he saw: and behold, the mountain was full of horses and chariots of fire round about Elisha (2 Kings 6:14-17).

Teaching them to observe all things whatsoever I have commanded you: and lo, I am with you alway, even unto the end of the world. Amen (Matthew 28:20).

ISN'T THAT a beautiful promise we have from the Lord: "Lo, I am with you alway"? I want to preach on *God's Abiding Presence.*

Loneliness can be an awful thing. Nobody likes to be alone. Everybody wants to have the feeling that he belongs to the group.

Loneliness can also be a very frustrating thing. It can take a person to the very depth of despondency and despair. In fact, the Communists often use this tactic to brainwash. They'll put a prisoner in a room all by himself—no furniture, no people, nothing. In one of those dingy, gray-colored rooms, over a period of time, his mind begins to do strange things. So, over a period of time, loneliness can actually snap a person's mind. It is a very heartbreaking thing.

The Lord said in the Book of Genesis, "It is not good that the man should be alone." Of course, He was referring to the physical aspect of husband and wife, but He meant more than that.

There is a difference in being alone physically and being alone spiritually. They are two different things entirely. A lot of folks are not alone physically, but they are alone spiritually.

There are several Biblical examples of what I'm trying to get across to you.

The number-one example is King Saul. Israel desired a king, so God said, "All right, I'm going to give you a king." So, there he was. He stood head and shoulders above all the people. King Saul, big and tall, strong, a man of war, a man of power. The Philistines would take one look at him, and get scared.

Saul led Israel to new heights of victory and glory. They even wrote songs about him, sang songs about him. He had plenty of followers.

The Bible says that at the beginning of Saul's kingship, the Lord gave him a new heart. (See, God's been doing it for thousands of years.) How do I know that? Because the Bible says that the Spirit of the Lord came upon Saul and he was turned into another man. That's how he started out. Oh, the Israelites were so proud of their king.

When they first put the crown on Saul's head, and arrayed him in royal purple, people's hearts swelled. "Why, there is no nation on earth that has a king as tall and broad-shouldered as Saul, our king. We're so proud of him, we're so happy because of him."

For awhile it was indeed beautiful. But when you consider Saul's life, you quickly see that it was not going to have a happy ending. Saul became proud of himself.

He fell in love with himself. He grew self-centered. He did not fully obey the voice of the Lord, therefore, God rejected him from being king over Israel. The Bible says that the Spirit of the Lord left Saul, and an evil spirit from the Lord troubled him.

In the latter part of Saul's life, we don't see the beauty that was there in earlier years. We don't see the humility that was there in the beginning. We see a man who had gone wild, a man who had gone berserk. Evil spirits had taken hold of him. He threw a javelin at David, trying to pin him against the wall and kill him. He even chased David through the forest with soldiers, and tried to hunt him out to kill him.

Something had happened to this man. He didn't have the tender spirit he had in that day when he was hidden among the stuff. And not only that. Something else had happened to him. He was a worried man. He was a man spiritually bankrupt and destitute. He was a man estranged from God.

I can see Saul many times, pacing the floor before a battle, saying to himself, "The Philistines have come, and are at my door. What am I going to do? The Lord doesn't speak to me any more. I don't have visions anymore. The prophets don't speak to me anymore; they just shake their heads. What's wrong, what's wrong?"

Here was a man who still had the respect of the people. He still had his armies, and they were standing behind him, saying, "Saul, we'll do whatever you say." The people still sang their songs. He was still surrounded by friends physically, but he was alone spiritually.

Finally, all alone in his tent, he said to himself, "I know what I'll do, I'll go down to the witch of Endor." He disguised himself, and put on strange clothes. You know why he disguised himself? Because, one of the first

things he had done when he became king was to put all
the witches out of the land. And now he was going to
visit one. He was embarrassed by the whole situation.
He disguised himself, for he didn't even want the witch
to know who he was. So he went to her house.

The witch asked, "What do you want?"

He said, "Call me up Samuel, I want to talk to the
man of God."

"He's dead, he's in the grave," she said.

"I know that, but call him up, I want to talk to him,
I've got to hear from God! I've got to hear from God!"

As a general rule, in such cases it was a demon that
would come forth and impersonate the person. But even
the witch herself was shocked this time, because God
allowed the spirit of Samuel himself to come up. It scared
even her. She jumped up and said, "You've deceived me.
You're Saul!"

"What do you see?" Saul asked.

"I see gods ascending out of the earth. I see an old man
coming up."

And Saul cried out in the dark of midnight. "Samuel,
Samuel, I've got to hear from the Lord. I don't have any
dreams or see visions anymore. The prophets don't speak
to me."

The voice came back from the prophet Samuel, who
was already dead, "By tomorrow at this time you'll be
where I am." In other words, "You're going to die tomorrow."

It's an awful thing to realize that Saul, Israel's first
king, went down to the grave, lonely, and in despair.
He went into battle the next day. He had his three sons
with him. They were killed by Philistines. Saul was
wounded in the battle and, in the midst of despair, he
fell on his own sword and committed suicide.

Did you know that twenty thousand people commit suicide each year in America? Twenty thousand people go the way of death, just as Saul did. That is because we are living in a nation of people who are estranged from God. They are lonely.

There is another example of what I'm talking about. In Babylon, there was a king by the name of Belshazzar. He said, "I'm going to throw a big party." We're going to drink, we're going to dance, we're going to have a big time." He invited more than a thousand of his friends, his lords, his maids. They drank, and the more they drank, the bolder they got. They danced and they laughed. Belshazzar was right there in the middle. He had the money, he had the influence, and they were all undoubtedly buttering him up. "Belshazzar, you're the best king we've ever had. No king in Babylon has ever thrown parties as good as the parties you throw."

But they went one step too far. They got the golden vessels that had been taken from the Temple in Jerusalem. "Let's drink wine out of them." They did. Thus they desecrated the vessels of God.

A few minutes later, the fingers of a man's hand appeared. What was it? I believe it was the hand of God. It began to write strange things on the wall of that building. Perhaps they didn't notice it at first. They were all dancing. Then someone noticed it, and then it was seen by the crowd. The people were astounded; they all stared.

Belshazzar wasn't smiling anymore. He wasn't dancing anymore. Here was a king who was shocked. He was scared. He had seen the fingers of a man's hand writing something on the wall.

Immediately, Belshazzar called for the magicians, the astrologers, the soothsayers, and all the wise men of Babylon. "Tell me what that means," he commanded. It was the most serious night in his life, and he knew it. He stood there in that large ballroom in front of more than a thousand people, and that man was alone. The astrologers couldn't help him, the magicians, the wizards and the soothsayers couldn't help him. The wise men were helpless. Here was a man who was terrified because he was without God.

Somewhere in your life you will come to the point where you will meet God. You might live fifty years and everything go your way, but eventually, sometime before you reach the grave, you'll come to a crisis, you'll come to a crucial point, you'll come to a time of chaos, you'll come to a moment of perplexity, you'll come to a place of consternation, you'll come to a place where you'll meet God. This will be a time when physical companionship alone will not satisfy your need. You'll need something beyond a father, something beyond a mother, something beyond a brother or a sister. You'll need a friend that sticketh closer than a brother. You'll need an ever-present help in the time of need. You'll need a rock. You'll need a shelter in the time of storm. You'll need Jesus, my Lord.

Someone told the king that Daniel could interpret dreams. They brought him into the king. The king asked him, "Can you interpret this?"

Daniel gave this interpretation: "Thou art weighed in the balances and art found wanting. Thy kingdom is divided and given unto the Medes and Persians." Belshazzar was slain that night. He never lived to see another sunrise. He had gone too far. God came to that party.

You may have ten thousand friends, but if God is not your friend, you'll go down to the grave in sorrow and regret.

I must have God as my friend. You can take the Kennedy's and the Rockefeller's as friends, but I'll take Jesus for mine.

Anyone without God is alone spiritually. Rich man, poor man, beggar man, thief—it doesn't make any difference. Anyone without God is alone. But, on the other hand, when we turn the record over and play the good side, the positive side, the Spirit of God side, we can safely say that Christians, the people of God, are never alone.

Think of how Stephen was stoned to death. They took him outside the city, for that's where people were stoned. He was away from his family, away from the church, away from his spiritual brothers and sisters. Saul was standing there, holding the coats of the men who were stoning him to death. And, so far as we know, Stephen had no one standing with him. His mother wasn't there, his brothers and sisters weren't there. His enemies were cursing him, beating him and throwing rocks at him, but in spite of all that lonely condition, Stephen was a man with a glow. I don't see a man down in the depth of despair; I see a man who is saying "Lord, lay not this sin to their charge. Lord Jesus, receive my spirit." Then the heavens were opened, and he saw Jesus standing on the right hand of God.

Go back to the time of David, as he faced Goliath. He **ran** forth to meet the giant. He didn't wait for the giant to be the aggressor. David had no spear, no shield, no sword, but he ran toward the giant.

Goliath cried out, "Why, you're just a boy. I'll give your flesh to the fowls of the air, and to the beasts of the field."

But David, in the midst of that giant's boasting, said, "You come to me with a spear, and with a sword and with a shield, but I come to you in the name of the Lord God of hosts whom thou has defied." He put a stone in his sling, slung it around, and the giant fell. David then took the giant's own sword and killed him. How could David be so courageous, when Saul himself, who stood head and shoulders above all the people, was so afraid? What was it about David that made him courageous and fearless? It was because he knew God was with him. He wrote in Psalm 23, "Yea, though I walk through the valley of the shadow of death, I will fear no evil: for thou art with me." The abiding presence of God makes all the difference in the world.

John the Revelator was the last of the Apostles; all the others had been martyred for the gospel message. He was more than ninety years old. About 96 A. D., the Roman Empire banished him, and exiled him to a lonely, deserted island called Patmos. He was so old, so loving and gentle, they probably thought he'd die of heart-break. But not so! He said, "I was in the Spirit on the Lord's day." Can't you see him on the island all by himself, having a prayer meeting, and the Spirit of God coming upon him. Perhaps the old fellow jumped up, threw his pen down, and did a little jig before the Lord.

In the Spirit on the Lord's day. That means on Sunday, but spiritually, it means he was actually transferred into the future, and it was the Lord's day. He was there, and witnessed it. Think of it! He was there, and wrote about it.

"What did you see John?" "Oh, I saw the glorified Jesus." "How many did you see?" "I saw one." "You didn't see two?" "No, I wasn't looking for two. I saw, in the midst of the golden candlesticks, one like unto the Son of man. I fell at his feet, because I knew who it was; it was Jesus, the image of the invisible God. All power was given unto him. I fell at his feet, and worshipped Him."

As human beings, we can't always determine who we're going to have as companions. Sometimes there are circumstances beyond our control. Sometimes we're forced to be away from home, maybe for a job or a special engagement. We might even have to go to a foreign country, where they speak a foreign language, where we won't know anybody and nobody will know us. We can't always determine who we're going to associate with physically. We might not always live in the same town with mother and father, brother and sister, son and daughter. We can't always determine our friendships physically.

But we do, as free moral agents, have the ability to decide for ourselves who we're going to have as a companion spiritually. And once companionship with God is established, there's not a demon in hell that can sever it. David said, "If I make my bed in hell, behold thou art there. If I ascend up into heaven, thou art there. If I take the wings of the morning, and dwell in the uttermost parts of the sea; even there shall thy hand lead me. . . . " This is the presence of God. It will be with us all the days of our lives.

This Holy Ghost is a wonderful "friend." If you receive the Holy Ghost, you will take it with you when you go out the door. It will be with you in the car, and when you lay your head on the pillow at night. It is the abiding presence of God. You can take it on the job with you. You might find yourself in an adverse situation or circumstance, but the Lord will be with you. This promise is only to the followers of the Lord, only to the children of God. Jesus said, "Lo I am with you alway, even unto the end of the world."

Let me take you back to a verse of my original text, 2 Kings 6:15. The man of God was Elisha. He was in a certain city, and had his servants with him. They got up early in the morning, went to the gate of the city and, behold, the enemy had surrounded the city and cut off every escape route. They had horses, chariots and instruments of war.

One servant, when he saw all the enemies, said, "We're doomed!" He said, "Master, they have us surrounded, and there is no way out. What shall we do?" You know what his problem was? He had eye trouble. He couldn't see spiritually. And all the time he was seeing negatively, and terrified, the man of God was standing there, cool, calm and collected. He prayed, "Lord, open his eyes that he may see." Suddenly the Lord opened the eyes of the young man and he saw, and behold, the mountain was full of horses and chariots of fire. He saw things in a different light. He saw the armies of God all over the place. The hills were full of them, round about the enemies of God.

Many people today have a negative attitude. I pray that God will open their eyes, that they may see.

Christians are never alone. Psalm 91:11, 12 says, "He shall give his angels charge over thee . . . They shall bear thee up in their hands, lest thou dash thy foot against a stone."

They put Paul and Silas in jail. But my Bible says that at midnight Paul and Silas prayed and sang praises unto God. Who feels like singing in jail? Who feels like praying in jail? Paul and Silas did, because they had God with them. There was a great earthquake so that the foundations of the prison were shaken. Every door was open, every chain fell off and every prisoner was set free. That was nothing less than the unadulterated power of God.

Anyone without God is alone. The song says:

> *Friendship with Jesus,*
> *Fellowship divine:*
> *Oh, what blessed sweet communion,*
> *Jesus is a friend of mine.*

Ephesians 4:5 says that there is "One Lord, one faith, one baptism."

Someone may say, "Now wait a minute. There is water baptism and there is Spirit baptism. Which one did Paul mean?"

You're not rightly dividing the Word of truth. Jesus said in John 14:20, "At that day ye shall know that I am in my Father, and ye in me, and I in you." That sounds like fellowship; that sounds like friendship.

Here is the fulfillment of this verse: When you're baptized in water in the name of the Lord Jesus Christ, actually you're being baptized into Jesus Christ. On the other hand, when you receive the baptism of the Holy Ghost, that is Jesus Christ, being baptized into you. So you are in him through water baptism and he's in you through Spirit baptism. You're in Him and He's in you. You gain this friend that sticketh closer than a brother, by obedience to the message of the new birth.

If you have not been baptized in Jesus' name, you don't know what you're missing. It's the wonderful thrill of a lifetime.

Everyone can be baptized in Jesus' name and filled with the Holy Ghost. It's for the young and it's for the old. I preached a certain revival, and on the first night a little girl of seven received the Holy Ghost. And in the same service a woman of eighty-three also received the experience. This proved to me that the promise is for everyone. It is for you and your children.

We are living in a prodigal generation. We are living in a generation that is turning to the zodiac, to the horoscope, to the astrologers, and even to the witches, simply because they can't reach God. God won't talk to them, because of their rebellion. This nation is estranged from God. People throughout America are alienated from God, their spirits are bankrupt and destitute.

Winston Churchhill, outstanding statesman, uttered these last words when he died in 1965: "I was bored with it all." Could it be that a man of his caliber and stature went through life, lived and died, lonely? With something lacking, something missing?

Marilyn Monroe deliberately took an overdose of sleeping pills at the age of thirty-three. People who are happy don't do those things. People who find satisfaction and joy in life don't kill themselves. Could it be that in spite of her fame and fortune, in spite of the fact that her name was in lights all over the country, she was still lonely?

I heard the story of a sixteen-year-old-girl in New York city. Her father was a famous and wealthy man. They lived in a swanky apartment house, fourteen stories above the ground. The parents came home one day and found that their daughter had jumped out the window, and had fallen fourteen stories to her death. They wept bitterly. They couldn't understand, because they had given this girl everything they could think of — money, a car, clothes. She was popular at school. Yet she took her own life. Before the girl jumped out the window, she wrote a note for her parents. She didn't say, "I love you," or "Good bye, Mom and Dad," or any of those usual things. The only words written on that piece of paper were, "Life was just not worth living."

Wouldn't that be a horrible memory to be left with.
"Dad, you failed. You gave me a car, you gave me money,
you gave me clothes, but, somehow, I realized something
was missing, and now I'm lost."

I say again that anyone without God is alone. Regardless of your position in life, regardless of your name, if
you are without God, you are alone.

Repent of your sins, be baptized in Jesus' name and
you'll be in Him. He will fill you with the Holy Ghost,
and He'll be in you. Then you'll have the friend that
sticketh closer than a brother; you'll have the abiding
presence of God.

THE HEAVENLY DOVE

And Jesus, when he was baptized, went up straightway out of the water: and, lo, the heavens were opened unto him, and he saw the Spirit of God descending like a dove, and lighting upon him (Matthew 3:16).

THIS MESSAGE involves the nature of the Holy Ghost. I want to talk about some things we need to know, not just in our heads, but in our hearts.

I wonder why the verse did not read, ". . . he saw the Spirit of God descending like a **hawk**." Or "like an **eagle**." These birds could have been chosen to be emblems of God's Spirit, but they were not chosen. Out of all species of birds, a dove was chosen.

I have done considerable research on doves, and I want to share a portion of this research with you.

Doves are found throughout the world — they are everywhere. This is representative of the Spirit of God. His Spirit is moving, not just locally, but universally.

Doves are monogamous. They mate for life. They live in strict "purity," and have eyes for only one mate. This, too, speaks of God's Spirit, for Jesus said, "And I will pray the Father, and he shall give you another Comforter, that he may abide with you forever" (John 14:16). When God filled us with the Holy Ghost, it was for life. He is not pleased with half-heartedness, lukewarmness or backsliding. Thank God for the Holy Ghost that will turn us around, and make us live for Jesus until He comes again!

Doves have no gall bladder, a thing which ornithologists say is unique among birds. The gall bladder is an internal organ that secretes a bitter fluid called bile, which supposedly counteracts poisons in the body. But God designed the dove without a gall bladder because He knew there would be no need for bitter fluid in its body, since no poison would be there.

How thankful we should be that there is no bitterness involved in the baptism of the Holy Ghost. There is nothing underhanded or deceptive about the experience. It is a wonderful Spirit! It is a marvelous Spirit!

A dove is the traditional symbol of peace. Perhaps this is true partially because this bird has a low, cooing voice.

Does not this also speak to us of God's Spirit? Once Elijah needed to hear from God. There was an earthquake, but God was not in the earthquake. There followed a whirlwind, but God was not in the whirlwind. Then there came a great fire, but God was not in the fire. After all these things, there came a still small voice, and spoke to Elijah. God help us to be in tune with that still small voice.

Doves have an amiable, affectionate disposition. This speaks of the truth that by the Holy Ghost we can have our hearts knit together in love.

When I was a small boy, I had a knit sweater. It would get caught on a nail, and would stretch way out of shape, but as soon as it was taken off the nail, it would come back together.

That is the way it should be in the kingdom of God. We have our differences, but if we are a people whose hearts are knit together in love, these things will not keep us apart.

Doves are mentioned often in poetry, as, for instance, in the Song of Solomon. They are associated with mourning and grieving. Doves are not aggressive, but are timid and gentle. Hawks and eagles are aggressive birds. They sweep down from high altitudes, snatch their prey in strong claws, and carry it off. But doves are not like this; doves are gentle. And everyone who has the Holy Ghost, and who yields to God's Spirit, will be gentle.

Jesus said to His disciples, "Behold, I send you forth as sheep in the midst of wolves: be ye therefore wise as serpents, and harmless as doves" (Matthew 10:16). There is nothing malicious about the Holy Ghost. There is nothing about it that gets into sweet people and makes them sour; it rather gets into sour people and makes them sweet. We are not "pickled" by the Holy Ghost; we are preserved until the day of redemption.

I would like to bring you some things which I have observed while on the evangelistic field.

First of all, the Holy Ghost is easily grieved. Paul said, "And grieve not the Holy Spirit of God, whereby ye are sealed unto the day of redemption" (Ephesians 4:30). A dove is a bird that is easily "grieved," and this is also true of the Holy Ghost. Therefore, we need to be careful how we behave as we walk with the Lord.

Sometimes I wonder how God can bless us as much as He does in Pentecostal services, in view of what goes on there. We have the reputation of being the strictest church in town when it comes to doctrine and standards of dress. But we often have the reputation of being the weakest when it comes to respect for the house of God.

God is not pleased with the gum-chewing in our churches. I think it is a shame that God has to compete with Wrigley's Spearment or Juicy Fruit chewing gum. We do not attend church to sit on a pew and look like a cow chewing its cud. We rather attend church to magnify the Lord, and to worship Him in spirit and in truth.

There is too much running around in many of our services today. We are offending the heavenly dove when we do that. I have been in places where there was so much running around that I felt I was preaching in a street meeting. I thought to myself, "One of these nights I'm going to get me a fistful of tracts, stand in the center aisle, pass them out, and invite people to 'come to church.'" We preachers know it is hard to hit a moving target.

The Bible says that the thief cometh not but for to steal. Some may not be faithful in attending church, but the devil attends regularly. He comes to fight, to bind, to hinder, to steal away God's blessings. But if we will come in one mind and one accord, we can defeat the devil, and see a great end-time revival.

Among other things, we need a revival of respect. We read of Abraham, Isaac and Jacob, but never of Abraham, Isaac and Esau. Why was Esau replaced by Jacob, the cutthroat, the conniver, the liar? It is well-known that the birthright actually belonged to Esau. But Esau had no respect for things spiritual. On the other hand, Jacob had a healthy respect for the things of God, the power of God, the unction of God. And may God give us respect for His house, His Word and His man.

Yes, the Spirit of God is easily grieved, easily vexed. Sometimes it is the small things that frustrate God's attempts to do what He really wants to do. For this reason we should come to church with the right purpose in mind. We are not coming to talk about Monday's wash or Wednesday's ironing. We are not coming to visit with a neighbor. We are coming to raise our hands and our hearts in worship to the holy God of heaven.

The Holy Ghost can be resisted. One of the most beautiful of all Bible stories is that of Abraham's sending his servant back to their native land to find a bride for his son, Isaac. After the long journey, the servant was divinely directed to a girl named Rebekah. He met the girl's family, and then asked her to come with him and be the bride of Isaac. The members of her family gathered around her, and asked, "Wilt thou go with this man?"

Think of the magnitude of the decision she was now called upon to make. She was being asked to leave father, mother, brothers and sisters, along with the familiar scenes of her homeland, and go with a stranger. But something in her heart said, "Go! Go! Go!" The voice was compelling; the Spirit of God was moving. So she said, "I will go."

What a beautiful type of the way God deals with people today. The servant is typical of the Holy Ghost that deals with men, moving, calling, wooing. This is taking place throughout the world, in every nation under heaven. God is knocking on heart-doors, calling people out of sin. Jesus said, "Behold, I stand at the door and knock: if any man hear my voice, and open the door, I will come in to him, and will sup with him, and he with me."

Yes, the Holy Ghost is calling people today to leave kindred, and the things of the world. But this call of the Spirit can be resisted, just as Rebekah could have resisted the invitation to be Isaac's bride.

The Holy Ghost can be quenched. Paul said, in 1 Thessalonians 5:19, "Quench not the Spirit." Just one verse with four words, but it is a big one. The word "quench" means to "put out." If we are not careful, all of us may well be guilty of this. We quench the Spirit when we fail to move in the direction God wants us to move. "As many as are led by the Spirit of God, they are the sons of God." May God give us strength and grace to follow the glory cloud all the days of our lives, until He returns from heaven, and takes us to be with Him.

What has happened to so much of our spontaneous worship? Have you noticed that we seem to have to resort

more and more to mechanics? Our preachers sometimes
have to be "cheerleaders," instructing the congregation:
"Say this, say that, stand up, sit down, do this, do that."
What has happened to spontaneous worship from the
heart?

If you are filled with the Holy Ghost, worship should
be second nature to you. Take your liberty! Enjoy yourself
in the presence of God!

The Holy Ghost can be withdrawn. Saul learned this
the hard way. He had the touch of God on his life, but
he lost it. Of him we read, "But the spirit of the Lord de-
parted from Saul, and an evil spirit from the Lord
troubled him" (1 Samuel 16:14).

I do not believe in the false theory of unconditional
eternal security. Some teach that once you have salvation, you'll always have it, regardless of what you do.
By disobedience, Saul lost God's Spirit, and so can you.
That same gentle dove that flew into your life can turn
around and fly out again. You need to covet God's Spirit,
desire it, entertain it, hold on to it, believe God for
more of it.

Psalm 51 is a penitential psalm of David. He prayed,
"Create in me a clean heart, O God; and renew a right
spirit within me. Cast me not away from thy presence;
and take not thy Holy Spirit from me." This should be the
prayer of our hearts, the burden of our souls. As individuals, we should pray, "Oh God, please don't ever let
me be guilty of losing that precious, tender touch of your
Spirit from my life." It can be lost, but, thank God, it
does not have to be.

The Holy Ghost can be blasphemed. People have asked,
"What is the unpardonable sin?" Jesus said, "And whosoever speaketh a word against the Son of man, it shall
be forgiven him: but whosoever speaketh against the

Holy Ghost, it shall not be forgiven him, neither in this world, neither in the world to come." That is it. When we speak of the Holy Ghost, we had better take our shoes off, for we are on holy ground. One may blaspheme Jesus, and be forgiven, but when he blasphemes the Holy Ghost, he is sure to spend eternity in the damnation of hell.

But what does it mean to blaspheme the Holy Ghost? Jesus had been casting out devils. The hypocritical, envious Pharisees admitted that devils were being cast out, but declared that Jesus was doing so by the power of Beelzebub, the prince of the devils. That is when Jesus warned against blaspheming the Holy Ghost.

When someone today says that the baptism of the Holy Ghost, with the evidence of speaking with other tongues, is of the devil, he is treading on thin ice.

I would like to turn now, and talk about the blessings of the Holy Ghost.

The baptism of the Holy Ghost is God's inward seal. According to 2 Corinthians 1:22, God ". . . hath also sealed us, and given the earnest of the Spirit in our hearts." And Paul said in Ephesians 4:30 that we are sealed by the Holy Ghost until the day of redemption. I call this "God's Seal of Good Housekeeping." When one repents, and is baptized in Jesus' name, thus cleaning up the "house," God gives him the Holy Ghost, thus stamping him with His seal of "good housekeeping." This is God's seal of approval.

The Holy Ghost baptism is also God's Spirit of adoption. Paul said, "For ye have not received the spirit of bondage again to fear; but ye have received the Spirit of adoption, whereby we cry, Abba, Father."

The story is told of a Jewish boy who boasted to a Gentile boy of his Jewish ancestry.

To this, the Gentile boy replied, "I have a more blessed

testimony than you."

"How is that?" the Jew asked.

The Gentile boy answered: "To begin with, you are a Jew outwardly, while I am a Jew inwardly. Then, too, you did not choose your nationality, but were born a Jew. You might say that God had to accept you as a Jew. But I am in the family of God by adoption. He chose me."

The baptism of the Holy Ghost can be described as "joy unspeakable and full of glory." Paul said, "For the kingdom of God is not meat and drink; but righteousness, and peace, and joy in the Holy Ghost."

The Bible speaks of the Holy Ghost baptism as a treasure in an earthen vessel. It makes us shout. It makes us weep. It makes us sing in the night. All these things, and many more, or mere samples of what is to come. They are the earnest of our inheritance. The full inheritance is yet to come. The river of life is yet to come. The tree of life is yet to come. The city of God is yet to come.

The Holy Ghost is the power to translate. It is God's resurrection power. The Father, the Spirit of the Son, and the Holy Ghost are all **one** Spirit. And the same Spirit that brought Jesus out of the grave is going to translate God's people from this planet. We are going to be Holy Ghost astronauts. We are going up in Jesus' name.

The Holy Ghost is the breath of God. Before His death, Jesus breathed upon the disciples, and said, "Receive ye the Holy Ghost." On the day of Pentecost, the mighty breath of God blew upon the waiting disciples, and they were all filled with the Holy Ghost.

In a sense, God exhaled at Pentecost. He will "inhale" at His second coming, and we shall all be caught away to meet Him in the air. It will be done by His Spirit, as Paul explained in Romans 8:11.

Paul described this glorious event in 1 Thessalonians

4:16, 17: "For the Lord himself shall descend from heaven with a shout, with the voice of the archangel, and with the trump of God: and the dead in Christ shall rise first. Then we which are alive and remain shall be caught up together with them in the clouds, to meet the Lord in the air: and so shall we ever be with the Lord."

THE NAME

And neither is there salvation in any other: for there is none other name under heaven given among men, whereby we must be saved (Acts 4:12).

THIS IS a message on the name of the Lord. I want to just preach about Jesus, to brag about Him a little bit. He's the one who is going to take us through. If He doesn't, nobody will.

The revelation of the name of Jesus is a progressive one. God did not, in the very beginning, fully reveal His name, His identity or His completeness. But, as Isaiah said, it was a matter of here a little and there a little, line upon line, and precept upon precept.

God started it by revealing Himself to Abraham as Elohim, a name that expresses the fulness of the divine nature. All the patriarchs, Abraham, Isaac and Jacob, knew God through what we call the Elohistic combinations. They knew Him as El Shaddai, which means the Almighty God. They knew Him as El Elyon, the most high God. They knew Him as a God who was high, lifted up, one that inhabited eternity, whose name was holy. They knew a majestic God, they knew a marvelous God. They served and walked with a God whom they believed created the heavens above and the earth beneath, the seasons, and all that was. They served the Almighty God, the everlasting God.

So far as the patriarchs went, that was the extent of the revelation at that time. Because this is the story: here a little and there a little, precept upon precept. These were holy men, but God didn't reveal Himself to just anybody. God is rather particular and choosy as to whom He reveals Himself. That's how sacred, that's how precious He is. So Abraham got a glimpse of God. He got a peek at the identity of the Lord.

Later, there was another man who was supposedly the meekest man who had ever lived. His name was Moses. He was a shepherd on the backside of the Midian desert for forty years, up to the age of eighty. One day he saw a strange sight. A bush was on fire and yet was not being consumed by that fire. The Bible says that he turned aside to see such a sight. As he approached that burning bush, an audible voice came out of it, called him by name, and said, "Moses, take your shoes off; the very ground you are standing on is holy ground. I am hereby ordaining and commissioning you to go unto Pharaoh and to be a leader among my people. You are to tell Pharaoh, 'Let my people go.'" Of course, Moses, being the meek man that he was, said, "But Lord, I'm nobody. Who am I? They won't believe me. Who shall I tell them sent me?"

The voice came back and said, "Moses, you go tell them I AM THAT I AM hath sent me unto you." We serve a God who is the great I AM. God always speaks of Himself in the present tense. He is not a great "I will be," or a great "I have been." He is not in the past tense or the future tense. We serve a God that is an ever-present help in the time of need. He is alive **now,** and he is full of love **now.** He is a miracle worker **now.** He is the I AM. He is a God of the present tense.

Well, God wasn't done with Moses yet. He worked him over again. They had a prayer meeting over there in Exodus chapter six. While Moses was praying, God spoke and said, "I appeared unto your fathers by the name of God Almighty, but by my name Jehovah, was I not known unto them." So there you have another revelation.

The name Jehovah is commonly regarded as God's Old Testament redemptive name. It means "God will save." That was the name which delivered Israel from Pharaoh, that was the name which redeemed them from Egypt's bondage.

God wasn't done yet. He continued to reveal Himself in divers places and at different times and to different ones through what is called the Jehovahistic Combinations. God revealed Himself unto David as **Jehovah-Raah,** "the Lord is my shepherd." He revealed Himself in one place as **Jehovah-Shammah,** which means "the Lord is there." He revealed Himself in another place as **Jehovah-jireh,** "the Lord will provide." When Israel fought against the Amalekites in the field of battle as they journeyed in the wilderness, God revealed Himself as **Jehovah-nissi,** which means "the Lord is my banner, or the Lord is my victory." Later, God revealed Himself as **Jehovah-Rapha,** "the Lord that healeth thee." Then He revealed Himself as **Jehovah-Tsidkenu,** the Lord is our righteousness. In another place He revealed Himself as **Jehovah-shalom,** "the Lord our peace." And then He revealed Himself as **Jehovah-Sabaoth,** which means "the Lord of hosts," or the God of battle, the undefeated, with a perfect, unblemished record. There are eight or nine of these Jehovistic combinations.

These revelations came to different men. Maybe it was Ezekiel or Jeremiah, or maybe it was some other prophet, but God was busy revealing Himself. It was a matter of here a little and there a little, precept upon precept, line upon line. The revelation of God was progressive. God didn't just jump out and say, "Well, here I am; you know everything about Me there is to know." No, He hid Himself, and revealed just little glimpses of Himself as He went along.

Keep in mind that while all of this was going on, while all these Elohistic and Jehovahistic combinations were being revealed, somewhere in heaven there was a big top secret being kept. It had been kept secret from the foundation of the world. There were several men in the Old Testament who tried to learn that name. Jacob was one of them when he wrestled with the theophany, and said, "What is your name?" the "man" wouldn't tell him. It was a question that was not answered because it wasn't time for the secret to come out.

Years later, the angel of the Lord appeared unto a couple, and told them of the coming birth of Samson. The man's name was Manoah. The angel did marvelous things in front of them, and before he left, they said, "Pray tell us what is your name, that we may honor you when the child is born." And he said, "Why is it that you ask my name, seeing it is secret?"

Surely God was revealing Himself, but don't you know that God always saves the best to the last? That's what that ruler of the feast said to the bridegroom at the wedding in Cana. "Why, you have kept the good wine until now" (last).

God always saves the best until last. In this dispensation, we're living in the day of God's best. If you don't get in on it, it is your own fault. God is making it available. I'm talking about experience. I'm preaching about the experience that God didn't hoard or keep to Himself. We're in a glorious dispensation.

God also saved the best for the last with respect to the revelation of His name. There was a secret being kept all that time, but I'm so glad that I can announce unto you that there came a time when God instructed His angel Gabriel to carry the secret down to a virgin named Mary, who lived in Nazareth.

When the angel appeared unto her, he not only came with greetings and salutations from God. He did more than that. He brought to light a name greater than any name that has ever been named, both in this world or in the world to come. He said, "Mary, the Holy Ghost shall overshadow thee, and thou shalt bring forth a son. Joseph is not going to name the boy; you're not going to name Him. This name was determined before the earth was ever created, this name was determined before the foundation of the world, to be the only name that would take away and remit sin. Thou shalt call His name Jesus, for He shall save His people from their sins."

The secret was out; it wasn't a secret anymore. The great Creator became our Savior. He that was rich became poor that we, through His poverty, might become rich. The divinity put on humanity, that humanity might share His divinity. He became a man, that we might lay aside the man and put on the Holy Ghost, put on Christ, and make it to heaven one day.

There is power in the name of Jesus. That's the name that folks were baptized in in the Book of Acts. That's the only baptism they had in the New Testament church. You cannot find where one person in the Bible was baptized in the titles, Father, Son, and Holy Ghost. It is not in there. Acts chapter 2, chapter 8, chapter 10, and chapter 19, all teach that they were baptized in some form of the name of the Lord Jesus Christ.

Out of all the Apostles, which one had the keys to the kingdom of heaven? Andrew? Philip? John? Who was it? Simon Peter. And he used them. He opened the door to the Jews in the second chapter of Acts. Later, he opened the door to the Samaritans (Acts 8). And then he opened the door to the Gentiles (Acts 10). In all three cases, he was in on it somewhere. In every case, they were baptized in the name of the Lord Jesus Christ, and they were filled with the Holy Ghost.

I believe that Matthew was right there, jumping up and down, clapping his hands, saying, "Amen! Preach it Peter." I don't believe there was any debate among them. Someone said, "I believe that there ought to have been a Peter-Matthew Debate." No, there was no need for that, because they didn't contradict one another. Peter fulfilled what Jesus commanded, and what Matthew wrote about.

They tell us that the Gospel of Matthew wasn't written until 62 A. D., and Pentecost was in 30 A. D. How do you think people were baptized for thirty-two years before there was any Matthew 28:19? I'll tell you: They were baptized in the name of the Lord Jesus Christ. If they weren't they just couldn't get into the kingdom. That's all there was to it.

I'm not afraid of Matthew 28:19. I love it; I'm all for it. Jesus said, "Go ye therefore, and teach all nations, baptizing them in the name of the Father, and of the Son, and of the Holy Ghost." That is a command. We are not to **recite** the command, we are to **obey** the command. That is where a lot of preachers make their mistake. They get over the candidate and say, "I now baptize you in the name of the Father, and of the Son, and of the Holy Ghost, and then **they don't do it.** They just "threaten" the candidate with it. There isn't any mention of the name involved. Instead of **obeying** the command, they are actually only **reciting** the command.

That would be like my telling you to go over and open the door. So what do you do? You go over to the door, and stand there and say, "Go open the door." You're just parroting what I said; you're not actually **obeying** what I said.

God doesn't want anyone to just repeat those words,

"Father, Son and Holy Ghost." Those are not names, they
are just titles. The command of Matthew 28:19 is fulfilled
in the use of the name of the Lord Jesus Christ. What is
the **name** of the Son? Is it "Son?" No! Then if this is not
the **name** of the Son, why should anyone use it in baptism. The name of the Son is Jesus. Matthew 1:21 said,
". . . thou shalt call His name JESUS: for he shall save
his people from their sins."

If the name of the Son is Jesus, then, pray tell, what is
the name of the Father? Maybe this verse will give you
a little hint: "Being made so much better than the
angels, as he hath by inheritance obtained a more
excellent name than they" (Hebrews 1:4).

What is your last name? What was your dad's last
name? You were born with the name you inherited from
your father. I didn't choose Smith or Jones or Roberts,
when I came into this world, I came with a name tagged
on me. My father determined what that name would be.
That name would be Willoughby.

By that same token, when Jesus Christ came into this
world, He said, "I am come in my Father's name. . . ."
(John 5:43). If the name of the Son was Jesus, then He
received the name by inheritance. You can put two and
two together. That should give you an idea what the
Father is saying. I believe that Jesus was God's Old
Testament secret name that was not fully revealed until
Bethlehem. Thank God, we can know it today as a saving
name, as a redemptive name, as a mighty name, as a
lovely name.

Even the name of the Holy Ghost is Jesus. Jesus said,
"But the Comforter which is the Holy Ghost, whom the
Father will send in my name, . . ." (John 14:26). Paul
said, ". . . which is Christ in you the hope of glory"
(Colossians 1:27). The Holy Ghost is the Spirit of Jesus

Christ. Jesus said in John 14:18, "I will not leave you comfortless: I will come to you." He said again ". . . for he dwelleth **with** you, and shall be **in** you."

Thank God, the Apostle Peter understood what that name was. That name was the Lord Jesus Christ. It is the only name under heaven given among men whereby we must be saved.

You might say, "Well, what difference does it make?" The next time your boss gives you your paycheck, turn the check over, write "son" on the back and try to get it cashed. If you're a father, write "father" on the back, and see if you can get it cashed. If you are a daughter, write "daughter" on the back, and see if you can get it cashed. No, the bank will reject all such endorsements, for those are just titles.

I'm a father, I'm a son, and I'm a minister, but I'm just one person. Even though I'm a father, that's not my name. And even though I'm a son, that's not my name. If I were to come into Tulsa International Airport and someone were to pick me up there at a certain time, someone who didn't know where I would be, he wouldn't get on the PA system, and say, "Would son please come to the American Airlines ticket counter." Why there are hundreds of sons out there. He would have to call for David Willoughby, and then I'd know that he was after me.

There is no authority in titles, but, praise God, there is the authority of heaven in the name of Jesus. The Bible says that at the name of Jesus, every knee shall bow, and that every tongue shall confess that Jesus Christ is Lord. If you don't bow now, you will later. If you don't confess now, you will later. Everybody is going to admit it sooner or later, but I'd rather do it sooner, than to be forced to do it later. I want to do it willingly. I love the name of Jesus.

When you are baptized in Jesus' name, your sins are remitted, never, never, to be brought up against you again. The name of Jesus erases it all.

I'm so glad for the name of the Lord, the strong and mighty tower. The righteous run into it and are safe. "Neither is there salvation in any other: for there is none other name under heaven given among men whereby we must be saved." What is that name? It is Jesus!

> *Sweetest note in seraph song,*
> *Sweetest name on mortal tongue;*
> *Sweetest carol ever sung,*
> *Jesus, blessed Jesus.*

It is the name that angels adore, and demons fear and dread before. I'm glad for the name of the Lord. I believe it is part of the gospel message.

You must be baptized in that name. The Bible teaches it. The encyclopedia teaches it. When the Bible was written, and in the days of the Apostolic church, baptism was always administered in the name of the Lord Jesus Christ. It was the Roman Catholic church that changed it. During the dark ages, and down through the centuries, this church has caused the wrong formula for baptism to be officially accepted and approved. It is not based on the Bible.

If you're going to be baptized, you ought to do it right. Let's go by the Book; what do you say?

The name of Jesus is tremendous; I can't say enough about it. He has a blessed name, a wonderful name, and He is just the same as His lovely name. We serve a great and mighty God.

I'm glad I know who Jesus is. I'm glad I know Him, not as the second person of the heavenly committee of three, but as the King of kings and Lord of lords.

If I were a trinitarian, I'd be embarrassed to even go to church on Easter Sunday, because I wouldn't be sure who raised Jesus from the dead.

I asked a trinitarian one time: "Who raised Jesus from the dead?"

He said, "Well, God the Father raised Him from the dead."

I quoted him Galatians 1:1, ". . . neither by man, but by Jesus Christ, and God the Father, who raised him from the dead." I took him over to John 2:19, where Jesus spoke of the temple of his body. He said, "Destroy this temple, and in three days, I will raise it up." I just kept smiling, and said, "Now who raised Jesus from the dead?" But I wasn't through yet. I took him over to Romans chapter 8:11, which says, "But if the Spirit of him that raised up Jesus from the dead dwell in you, he that raised up Christ from the dead shall also quicken your mortal bodies by his Spirit that dwelleth in you." That tells us that it was the Holy Ghost that raised Jesus from the dead. I just kept smiling, and then I said, "Now, who raised Jesus from the dead?"

Don't tell me that it took three different ones to get Him out of the grave. Wouldn't it have been rather embarrassing if the Father had shown up to raise the Son from the dead, and the Son had said, "Wait a minute! What are You doing here? I said I'd do it." And the Holy Ghost had elbowed His way in, and said, "Wait a minute! You're both wrong. I said I'd do it." Then the Father had said, "No! Don't you remember? I said specifically that I would raise Him from the dead."

I don't believe there were any arguments in the Godhead on the first Easter Sunday morning. On that great resurrection morning, he raised Himself from the dead by the power of God the Father.

God is a Spirit. There is but one God, and that God manifested Himself as the Father in creation, as the Son in redemption, and as the Holy Ghost in the infilling experience. That ought to make sense to anybody.

If there were a trinity, its members would be guilty of keeping secrets from one another. Luke 10:22 says, ". . . no man knoweth who the Son is, but the Father; and who the Father is, but the Son, and he to whom the Son will reveal him." That doesn't even mention the Holy Ghost. He's out in the cold. Then over in Mark 13:32, it says "But of that day and that hour knoweth no man, no, not the angels which are in heaven, neither the Son, but the Father." If the Father, Son and Holy Ghost are three separate persons, that means there are at least two things the Holy Ghost doesn't know, and one thing the Son doesn't know.

Revelation 19:11, 12 talks about Jesus Christ coming back riding on a white horse, clothed with a vesture dipped in blood, and on it a name written which no man knoweth but He Himself. That makes about three things the Holy Ghost doesn't know, one thing the Father doesn't know, and one thing that the Son doesn't know. So if there are three separate persons in the Godhead, none of them is capable of knowing all things, and they are all guilty of keeping secrets from one another.

I'm glad for the great gospel light. I'm glad for the day that the Holy Ghost comes along, rolls the curtain back and you see Jesus Christ. Flesh and blood cannot reveal it unto you, but it takes the Father which is in heaven.

This Jesus I'm talking about is wonderful. He is all together lovely. He has a name above all others, and He is absolutely fantastic.

Someone said to me, "He can be just about anything

you want him to be," and that's true. He is versatile. To the astronomer, He is the bright and morning star. To the architect, He's the sure foundation. To the builder, he's the door. To the banker, He's the owner of the cattle on the thousand hills. To the baker, He's the living bread. To the bride, He is the bridegroom. To the doctor, He is the great physician. To the educator, He is the wisdom and knowledge. To the farmer, he is the Lord of the harvest. To the horticulturist, He is the true vine. To the jury, He is the judge of all men. To the philosopher, He is the truth. To the lawyer, He is the advocate with the Father; Christ Jesus the righteous, winning our case with His own blood. To the soldier, He is the sword and shield. To the sailor, He is the master of the sea. To the traveler, He is the way. To the florist, He is the lily of the valley and the sweetest rose of Sharon. To the mortician, He is the resurrection. To the sinner, He is the Lamb of God that taketh away the sins of the world. To the geologist, He is the rock of ages and to the zoologist, He is the Lion of the tribe of Judah. To the seeker, He is the Holy Ghost.

There is nobody, dead or alive, who can be compared with my Jesus. You may name me someone who was great in one field, and I'll name you someone in that same field who was equally as great. Examples would be—in baseball, Babe Ruth and Lou Gehrig; music, Beethoven and Mendelssohn; prophets, Elijah and Elisha; spiritual leaders, Moses and David. Match them stride for stride, accomplishment for accomplishment. Nobody has ever stood alone; everyone has had his equal somewhere down the line. You name someone in any category, and there came along someone else who equaled him.

But when I mention the name of Jesus, I mention someone who stands alone, and there is none that you

can put beside Him. There is nobody in front of Him,
behind Him, or beside Him. There is none equal to Him.
There is nobody to be compared with Him. Thank God,
He is the highest person I know. He is the most magnifi-
cent one I know.

Several years ago, over in Saudi Arabia, a Christian
encountered a Mohammedan priest. This priest had a
rosary hanging around his neck, and on that rosary
there were one hundred and sixteen beads. Each one
of those beads stood for a name or a title of his god, Allah.
When he encountered that Christian, he began to rattle
those names, all one hundred and sixteen of them. When
he got through, he looked at that Christian, and said,
"All right, now I'm done, it's your turn. What have you
got to say about your Jesus?"

The Christian had to hang his head, because he couldn't
think of too many things to say about his Lord.

All I can say is that I wish I had run into that Mohammedan priest. My study is not complete, but not long
ago I began to make a personal survey on the titles and
the names of the Lord Jesus Christ that are mentioned
in the Bible. I want to give you a few of these, so you will
have a general idea of what the Bible has to say about
your Lord and Christ. I have scripture for every one of
these.

Jesus is the last Adam, He's the advocate, He's the
Almighty, He's the Alpha and Omega, He's the author
and finisher of our faith, He's the bread of life, He's the
beginning and the end, He's the captain of our salvation,
He's the chief shepherd, He's the chief cornerstone, He's
the counselor, He's the Creator, He's the Comforter, He's
the deliverer, He's the everlasting Father, He's the
eternal God, He's the good shepherd, He's the image of
God, He's the King of kings, He's the law-giver, He's

the Lamb of God, He's the lion of the tribe of Judah, He's the Lord of lords, He's the resurrection and the life, He's our passover, He's the Son of righteousness, He's our shield, He's the true vine, He's the faithful witness, and He's the Word of God.

You can talk about Mohammed and Confucius, but they can't hold a light to my Jesus. You may say that Buddha and Mohammed did great and mighty deeds. So what! My Jesus brought freedom to the captive. He took away their ashes and gave them beauty. He unstopped deaf ears, opened blind eyes, and healed all manner of diseases and sickness.

You say, "Mohammed not only lived for what he believed; he even died for what he believed." So what! So did my Jesus. He went to Calvary and died for people like you and me.

You say, "Mohammed was buried, and his shrine is among us even today." Jesus was also buried, and His shrine is visited by hundreds of thousands of people every year.

But that's where the comparison ends. Buddha, Mohammed and Confucius may have lived good lives, and said and did great things. Then they died, were buried, and their bodies turned to dust. But my Jesus did something on that third day after He was in the grave that no Buddah, no Mohammed, no Confucius ever did. He arose, and He is living in the hearts of His people. He is alive forevermore. He is the mighty God, the everlasting Father, the Prince of Peace.

In the early days of Pentecost, the devil fought the Azusa Street revival. A black man by the name of W. J. Seymour was sitting behind two orange crates one night, praying. Two rowdy boys came in, trying to break up the meeting. Brother Seymour just quietly and calmly got up from behind the crates, walked up to the pulpit, pointed his finger at those boys and said, "I bind you in the name of the Lord Jesus Christ." God froze them right there on the floor. They couldn't move one muscle. The name of Jesus is a name to be reckoned with.

A few years later, two preachers saw the light on baptism in Jesus' name, and they baptized one another in that name. Their names were Frank Ewart and Glenn Cook.

Glenn Cook, a famous evangelist, went to St. Louis to preach, and from there he went on to Indianapolis. This was the home of the noted preacher, G. T. Haywood.

J. Roswell Flower, who was then General Secretary-Treasurer of the Assemblies of God, wrote to Brother Haywood that Glenn Cook was headed for Indianapolis with the erroneous, "new issue" doctrine. To which Brother Haywood replied, "Your warning came too late; I have already been rebaptized." He soon baptized his entire church, 465 members, in Jesus' name.

Still later, Andrew Urshan stood up one night and preached about the mighty God in Christ. While he was still preaching, God confirmed it with signs following. One woman sitting in the congregation got up, shook her fist at him, and said, "You will die for giving that kind of a message." She went out the door immediately, and didn't even stay to hear the complete message. She was struck down by a vehicle, and was killed.

The name of Jesus is not a name to take lightly. It is not a name to cast aside or reject. It is a name to love and to cherish and hold dear to your heart. Take the name of Jesus with you. If you will fall in love with the name of Jesus, if you will fall in love with the lovely Lord, and worship Him and praise Him, He will give you the desires of your heart.